MASTER OF WAR

MASTER

OF

WAR

Blackwater USA's
ERIK PRINCE
and the Business of War

Suzanne Simons

HARPER

An Imprint of HarperCollins*Publishers*
www.harpercollins.com

HarperCollins books may be purchased for educational, business, or
sales promotional use. For information, please write:
Special Markets Department, HarperCollins Publishers,
10 East 53rd Street, New York, NY 10022.

FIRST EDITION

Designed by Jennifer Ann Daddio/Bookmark Design & Media Inc.

Library of Congress Cataloging-in-Publication Data
Simons, Suzanne.
Master of war: Blackwater USA's Erik Prince and the
business of war / Suzanne Simons.
p. cm.
ISBN 978-0-06-165135-9
1. Prince, Erik, 1969– 2. Blackwater USA. 3. Businessmen—
United States—Biography. 4. Private military companies—United States.
5. Mercenary troops—United States. 6. Mercenary troops—Middle East.
7. Iraq War, 2003—Economic aspects. 8. Afghan War, 2001—
Economic aspects. I. Title.
UB148.S54 2009
956.7044'31—dc22
2008054005

09 10 11 12 13   OV/RRD   10 9 8 7 6 5 4 3 2 1

Dedicated to

Kira, Finn, Ryan, Stefan, and Rita.

Thank you for your uncompromising love and support.

CONTENTS

ERIK PRINCE'S BODY bounced off the hood of the North Carolina Parks Department pickup truck before vanishing over a steep embankment next to a mountain road.

He had been going so fast that he couldn't control the bike, couldn't steer it out of the truck's path in time. Prince's longtime friend Chris Burgess watched, horrified.

Prince and Burgess had signed up as a two-man, under-forty team for the annual Special Operations Adventure Race, an incredible test of endurance and physical strength. Participants spend anywhere from five to ten hours biking, paddling, rappelling, and running through the western mountains of Highlands, North Carolina. Prince and Burgess had gone through Navy SEALs training together several years earlier. Since then, Burgess had come to work for Prince as one of nearly a dozen vice presidents at Prince's private military company, Blackwater. Prince ran Blackwater much like a military unit, and he and his top lieutenants all worked to maintain their physical conditioning. Prince often paired up with his men in tests of strength and endurance much like this North Carolina race.

The two had just finished rappelling down a mountain and had hopped on their bikes for a downhill sprint. Burgess—who was in front of Prince—saw the pickup truck coming toward them first. He knew he was going too fast and tried to apply his brakes without losing control of his mountain bike. He made a lane switch at the last moment that took him out of the path of the oncoming truck. Prince did not. Burgess turned his head just in time to see Prince collide head-on with the truck.

"All I saw is this flash of him going by," said Burgess. "I thought, Oh, man, I just killed the boss."

Prince hit the front fender of the truck, slammed onto the hood, and then catapulted some twenty-five feet down an embankment. He just missed slamming into a tree before coming to a halt. He lay motionless on the ground that was covered with pine needles, leaves, and rocks.

Miraculously, he had avoided serious injury. He took a mental inventory of all of his parts. "Everything was working, so I thought OK, great, get up," said Prince.

The two parks department employees had gotten out of their truck with a look of sheer horror on their faces. With Burgess, they stood in amazement as Prince climbed up the embankment and asked where his bike was. The Cannondale had been a present from his wife, the last gift she had given him before her death four years earlier. It was among Prince's most-prized possessions.

The bike hadn't been as fortunate in the collision as Prince had been. It sat off to the side of the road, mangled and bent. Pumped full of adrenaline, Prince waved off concerns about his injuries and focused on the bike. Could it withstand the remaining six to seven hours of the race?

"We spent about twenty minutes jumping up and down on the back fork of the bike, which was so bent," said Burgess. "Finally, we were able to straighten it out, but it still had a one-inch wiggle."

With the effects of the adrenaline wearing off and the pain starting to set in, Prince hopped back on his bike, determined to finish the race. Every time his rear wheel turned, it dragged against the fork, eventually wearing a hole right through it. Yet Prince was not going to call it a day; he wasn't going to quit in front of Burgess. They made it to the finish, not as fast as some of the younger Special Ops contestants, but in impressive time for two guys pushing forty.

Prince's entire life, and certainly his astonishing career at Blackwater, had been something of an adventure race. Sprint at top speed, crash occasionally, but never stop racing. Sometimes it meant cutting corners. Sometimes it meant leaving slower team members behind. Prince had relied on persistence and determination to grow Blackwater from little more than a training facility for military Special Operations and law enforcement personnel into a billion-dollar powerhouse, with the U.S. government as his largest client. The company had provided an ever-expanding list of services that included personal protection of U.S. diplomats in Iraq, security services at fixed locations for some of the CIA's most sensitive sites around the world, and airlift support for the Department of Defense in places like Afghanistan and Pakistan.

Blackwater designed and built its own weapons and aircraft, and purchased many, many more. It has a massive Rolodex of some forty thousand former military and law enforcement personnel at its beck and call. Prince built a private spy service. It operated in over a dozen countries. And it is all owned entirely by its founder, Erik Prince.

But Blackwater's breakneck growth brought with it a host of problems. The company's relentless determination to meet a growing demand for military services all over the world sometimes led to rules being broken.

While Prince likely would have preferred that his company remain a stealth operation, the images of his men being brutally murdered and dragged through the streets of Fallujah in 2004 made that impossible. Pictures of two of his employees dangling from a bridge spanning the Euphrates River was how much of the world was introduced to Blackwater. Four years later, in the fall of 2007, Blackwater men killed a host of Iraqi civilians in a Baghdad traffic circle. That is how the world got to know Prince himself, as the incident landed him before Congress and the media. It also touched off a slew of investigations and forced the U.S. government to take a closer look at how it managed private companies.

Beginning in 2003, after the invasion of Iraq, the rise of private military companies like Blackwater has been nothing less than meteoric. Private contractors now occupy the battlespace in Iraq on a one-to-one ratio with U.S. troops. They are often paid a lot more money by the taxpayer, and they aren't governed by the same rules as U.S. troops. The stark lack of oversight and accountability of the industry has led to numerous congressional hearings and has put the policies of the Bush administration into question. Has the United States government farmed out too many critical parts of its own mission? Who will police this growing shadow army?

In the case of Blackwater, there are many more questions to add to these. How did the company win its big contracts? Whom does it employ, within the United States and abroad, through its various subsidiaries? Why were its men caught in Fallujah? What does Prince's spy service do, and for whom?

The answers to all of these questions go back to one man: Erik Prince.

In just ten years, Prince had gone from small business owner to major Washington powerhouse. He had built his empire in part on his own personal wealth—which is substantial—derived from a windfall inheritance from his father. But he also built it through the aggressive pursuit of lucrative private-sector solutions for some of the world's stickiest problems. He controled a private army that could single-handedly win many small wars. Is he a business genius? A war profiteer? The lucky recipient of a government shell game? What makes him tick?

Over the course of eighteen months, during which he granted more than one hundred hours of interviews and access to Blackwater's top offices and facilities around the world, he gave me the chance to find out.

CHAPTER 1

The Prince

ERIK PRINCE LEARNED A LOT from his father—both from his life and from his death. Edgar Prince was just a boy when his own father died of a heart attack at the age of thirty-six. The death left young Edgar with little choice but to assume a new identity as caretaker for his widowed mother and two siblings. Edgar Prince would eventually build a fortune, but he would do it on a history of hardship.

"They made it through the Great Depression and through the war," recalled Erik. Not even a teenager, Edgar worked his way through middle school by taking a job at a local car dealership, where he cleaned and prepped new vehicles for delivery.

By the time Edgar was old enough to go to college, money was still tight, so he joined the military to help him get through. When he left college, he served his two-year commitment in the Air Force. The military was never a passion for Edgar, the way it would be for his son.

Edgar Prince was a man driven by business. After the Air Force, he took a job at an automotive supplier in western Michigan. He worked in multiple departments, learning everything from sales to research and development. Erik believes that that wide-ranging experience is a big part of the reason that, when the company changed hands and Edgar didn't get on well with the new management, he decided it was worth the risk to go out on his own.

By 1965 Edgar Prince had collected close to $160,000 to launch a small die-cast shop he called Prince Manufacturing. He based the company in his hometown of Holland, Michigan.

"Six guys came with him," remembered Erik. "He mortgaged his house, his car, about anything you could mortgage. His mother, as a single mom in the '30s, '40s, and '50s, had managed to save $10,000, and she invested that in the company."

It was a tremendous financial risk for a man with a young family to support. Erik's mother, Elsa, remembered just how hard it was. "We were so frugal, I would write down in my pocketbook if I bought a spool of thread or stamps," said Elsa. "That's how closely we kept our records."

But not everyone believed that Edgar Prince's decision was a smart one. There was fierce competition in automotive manufacturing in Michigan in the mid-1960s, and several larger companies were already heavily invested in the marketplace. Erik recalls a talk his father gave about the company years later, when he told employees of the hurdles he once faced.

"All the smart people, all the businesspeople," Erik remembered his father saying, "they said, 'You really shouldn't start a capital-intensive business like this with anything less than $5 million.' My dad said, 'Well, if I had $5 million, I wouldn't be trying to start a business right now, I'd be hanging out.'"

The potential for failure drove Edgar to work harder, which

often meant long days away from his family. "We knew that in small businesses, two out of three fail, and his could have failed," recalled Elsa.

Edgar and Elsa Prince already had three daughters by the time Erik was born in 1969. The family was deeply rooted in their conservative Dutch community, and Prince's company hired many of its employees from among the local population. Prince Manufacturing was well on its way to becoming Holland's largest employer. Even today, visitors to downtown Holland are greeted by the bronzed footsteps of Edgar Prince that lead to a statue of musicians near a plaque that reads, "We will always hear your footsteps."

But much like what had happened to his own father, all of Edgar Prince's hard work would come at a price. One day, when Erik was just a toddler, his father came home in the middle of the day and went straight to bed. Erik knew something was terribly wrong.

"That just never happened," Prince said. "I was scared. My mom took him to the hospital, and he ended up having a heart attack there, which probably saved his life."

Edgar began a recovery process that took weeks, but almost immediately, his family noticed a change. With more time to think about his life, he began to shift some of his priorities. Elsa saw Edgar become a man of renewed faith, saying not only did the heart attack change her husband's life, but "he just realized he could be gone, and what do you leave?"

Edgar Prince's relationship with God had always been important to him, but it rose to a new level after his heart attack. Edgar believed that God had given him a second chance, and it must be for a reason. The elder Prince made changes in his life that would almost immediately benefit Erik. Father and son spent more time together, making little lead soldiers and crafting pieces for chess games. Edgar even built his son an air hockey table after seeing one on a trip to Disney World in Florida.

"I think he tried to relax a little bit more," recalled Erik. "He was still pushing the business, but I think he gave some of the other guys a bit more free rein, and some great things started to happen."

One of those "things" was a dramatic shift within the company from making machinery to making parts. It was another risk Edgar was willing to take. Erik insists that finding more efficient ways to do things is what drove his father, even though some of his ideas weren't exactly show stopping. Not all of them had to do with cars, either. A propeller-driven snowmobile and a ham deboning machine were just two of Edgar Prince's earlier experiments that didn't exactly take off.

"The ham deboning machine was a great product," said Erik. "My dad says in Bulgaria, at one point, we had 100 percent market share in ham deboning machines."

It was in the early 1970s that Edgar Prince's company came up with a very simple product that would have a dramatic impact on the automobile industry. Prince engineers patented an automotive sun visor that could light up.

"They sold the first 5,000 to General Motors before they ever made one," said Prince. "They figured out how to make them fast, and when the business was sold, they were making 20,000 a day."

The sun visor became a staple of the automotive industry that led to a financial windfall for the Prince family. It was a classic American small-business success story, and with the company's success, the Prince family solidified its role as a leading fixture of its tight-knit community.

As the youngest of four children, Edgar and Elsa's only son spent a lot of time by himself. His sisters, Betsy, Emilie, and Eileen, were quite a bit older than Erik, and there weren't a lot of kids his age in the Princes' affluent neighborhood. Erik had picked up a passion for the outdoors from his cousins and found that being outside surrounded by nature was a place where he felt at home.

"I learned to trap, self-taught," Erik recalled. "I spent a lot of time with a BB gun and a hatchet."

By the time he was in middle school, Prince was getting up extra early before heading off to classes so that he could check his traps. It might not be the kind of hobby you'd expect to find in a deeply religious family, but Erik's mother called his love of hunting "a gift of the Lord, because his father was totally, totally different and was not interested in hunting or guns or any of that."

But there were some interests that father and son would share, among them a passion for learning more about the world. Before Erik was ten years old, he had seen firsthand the places where some of history's worst atrocities had occurred, including a trip through Europe and a visit to one of the most notorious Nazi death camps of World War II.

The Nazi government called Dachau the first concentration camp for political prisoners, but it also held members of trade unions, Jehovah's Witnesses, homosexuals, Roma (Gypsies), and, beginning in late 1938, an increasing number of Jews. More than ten thousand Jewish men were sent to Dachau in late 1938 and early 1939, where they were forced to work under slave labor conditions. It is believed others were used as human guinea pigs for Nazi medical experiments. When American troops liberated Dachau in 1945, they discovered dozens of railroad cars filled with dead bodies. The realization of what had occurred there made a lasting impression on Prince, as did a visit to the beaches of Normandy.

"It made a big impression," recalled his mother. "Young men had died for our freedom, and I think as he was growing up as a teenager, it really bothered him the way young people just took it for granted and even rebelled against the country. He would just say, 'They don't know what they have.'"

On Erik's seventh birthday, his family visited Berlin, half of which was still behind the Iron Curtain.

"Seeing guns and dogs, tanks and mine traps, all facing in, keeping people in East Germany—that had a forming effect on me," Prince recalled. Among other things, it taught him that communism was bad and that the free market democracy he was raised in was good. It also helped solidify his interest in military and international affairs.

A STRONG BELIEF IN GOD was also a significant part of Erik Prince's childhood. "I was raised in a churchgoing home," said Prince. "I went to church on Sunday. I went to Christian schools, run by the Christian Reformed Church. It's just the denomination I was raised in."

The Christian Reformed Church was rooted in the Dutch Reformed Church, with many of its members sharing Dutch heritage. It was also a closely knit community, even among third- and fourth-generation Dutch Americans. Pastor Albertus van Raalte fled the Netherlands and settled in the United States around Holland, Michigan, in 1848. He held closely to the teachings of John Calvin, who preached, among other things, the concept of predestination: the belief that nothing one does in this life will take one from the hand of God. But in 1857 the Christian Reformed Church officially broke from the Dutch Reformed Church, disagreeing with the latter's state establishment.

While Prince described his faith as fairly typical, his was not a usual religious upbringing. As their wealth grew, Edgar and Elsa Prince made generous donations to religious causes they believed in. They made fast friends among prominent evangelicals, many of whom became dinner guests in the Prince house. Most of them shared the same conservative values that the Princes taught their children.

James Dobson, founder of the conservative advocacy group Focus on the Family, became a good family friend, as did Charles Colson, who had once served as special counsel to President Richard Nixon. Colson had once been known as the "hatchet man" and the "evil genius" in the Nixon administration because of his dirty dealings with political opponents. After the Watergate break-in in June 1972, Colson pled guilty to obstruction of justice in a Watergate-related case. He served seven months in prison and went on to found the Prison Fellowship in 1976, reinventing himself as a man of God. The nonprofit organization counseled prisoners and ex-prisoners in finding a path to Jesus Christ, and later grew to become one of the largest prison ministries in the world. In 2005 *Time* magazine named Colson one of the Twenty-Five Most Influential Evangelicals in America.

Elsa Prince knew her children were getting an upbringing that was well out of the reach of most families. "We were members of several different groups," recalled Elsa. "We would go and hear different people speak at the Republican Leadership Council, which was led by our congressman, Guy Vanderjack, at that time. Erik and his sisters were exposed to a lot, probably way more than an average student, and it was just an opportunity that we had that some of the other children didn't."

Gary Bauer, president of the conservative group American Values, also became close friends with Edgar and Elsa Prince. The public policy group advocated against abortion and in support of traditional marriage. Bauer, speaking about the Prince family to the *New York Times,* said, "They are conservative Christians, and they have very strong views on the sanctity of human life and the defense of marriage and the role of faith in the public square."

There was little doubt that the family was rooted in conservative Republican values. And their influence was growing. In the late 1970s, Erik's older sister Betsy married Dick DeVos, son of billionaire Richard DeVos. The elder DeVos had earned millions as the cofounder of Amway, a multilevel marketing business. Both Betsy and her husband went on to play a prominent role in Michigan politics; Betsy supported several Republican initiatives and served as chair of the Michigan Republican Party, while Dick ran unsuccessfully for governor of Michigan on the Republican ticket in 2006.

WHILE ENJOYING THE BENEFITS that came with being part of the influential Prince family, Erik was also fiercely determined to prove himself. By the time he was a teenager, it was painfully clear that once he set his mind to something, he rarely backed down. Having flown on his father's company planes as a little boy, Prince had developed a passion for aviation, and before he could even drive, he began studying to earn his pilot's license.

"I started taking lessons when I was fifteen, which is the earliest you can do it," recalled Prince. "I soloed on the morning of my sixteenth birthday. I soloed three airplanes: a Cessna 152, 172, and 182."

By the time he turned seventeen, Erik Prince was a pilot. Determination and the ability to focus intently on his goals set him apart from some of the other kids at Holland Christian High School, where he also became an athlete, running track, playing soccer, and wrestling. "I played three sports a year pretty much every year," Erik recalled, adding that he lettered in track his freshman year. His soccer team won the state championship in its division his senior year, and Prince was noticed as much for his disposition as for his athletic ability. Others would later remember him as the kid who would stay late after an event to help clean up.

But while Prince benefited from his family's prominent place in the small community, he didn't always feel comfortable flaunting it. His mother says Erik wanted to be recognized on his own merits, not because of his family's wealth.

"Every year we got a new car because we had to, that was our business, and Erik wanted the oldest, rumbly, old Wagoneer that we had, and that's what he wanted to drive," recalled his mother. "If he had to drive with his dad, he wanted to be dropped off at the corner. Rather than try to show off, he wanted to be just one of them."

Even in high school, Prince was always thinking about what came next. It seemed a natural fit to combine his interest in the military with his love of flying.

"I wanted to be a military pilot really before I knew anything about the SEAL teams," said Prince. "I went and visited both the Naval and Air Force academies."

He entertained the idea of following in his father's Air Force footsteps and applied to the Air Force Academy, but the Naval Academy was ready to accept him first. Prince had set his mind on becoming a sailor, when he got a call from Democratic Senator Carl Levin.

"Lo and behold, Senator Levin's office called and said we want to appoint Erik to the Air Force Academy," said Elsa.

But Prince had made up his mind. He was going to the U.S. Naval Academy.

PART OF THE MISSION of the United States Naval Academy in Annapolis, Maryland, is to develop midshipmen "morally, mentally, and physically." The focus on discipline was one of the things that attracted Prince to the four-year program.

By the time Erik was nineteen, he already had very strong ideas about how things should be. He was led by a sense of right and wrong ingrained in him by his parents and those around them, and he had trouble reconciling mission and reality when he arrived at the academy.

"There was a lot of drinking going on," his mother said, "a lot of drinking. Erik was always very self-disciplined, and this really bothered him. These were supposed to be the cream of the crop, and here they were drinking away. And it was a time when women were coming onboard, and the use and abuse of women—he just didn't like it."

But it was fallout from a three-day leave he took as a sophomore that proved too much for Prince to tolerate. Edgar and Elsa traveled to White Sulphur Springs, Montana, to attend a conference, and Erik came along for the ride, hoping to enjoy a long weekend in the outdoors.

In many ways, Montana's Smith River valley was the ideal getaway for an outdoorsman. Nestled between Yellowstone Park and Glacier Park, the little town, surrounded by the Castle Mountains to the east, Little Belt Mountains to the north, and Big Belt Mountains to the west, seemed the perfect place for Prince to unwind.

Erik and his parents were guests at a ranch house that belonged to friends. On a Saturday night, Erik went for a run and was in a hurry to clean up before dinner. He struggled with the old-style porcelain handle in the shower. It wouldn't budge, so he pushed harder, this time with enough strength to shatter the handle.

The cuts to his right hand and thumb were deep.

"There was no feeling in my thumb, and I couldn't bend it at all because the tendon was severed," Prince recalled.

He knew the cut would require medical attention, so his dad took him to the local clinic.

Downtown White Sulphur Springs didn't look much different than it had in 1886 when James Brewer decided to develop the town as a stage stop. The road was paved now, but the small, nondescript, boxy buildings that lined the main street looked like something from another era. Prince arrived at the medical clinic before the doctor did.

"I'll never forget the cowboy doctor who drove up in a huge old Suburban with big mud tires and a cow pusher kind of rack on the front. He came in with his boots on and a huge belt buckle, big belly hanging out, and he just stitched me up. There wasn't a lot of focus on nerve connectivity or anything like that; he just put some stitches in and said, 'Ah, you'll be fine.'"

Prince was less than confident in the medical care. It wasn't what he was used to. The next morning, his father began making calls back home to Michigan. Prince had hurt his right hand and thumb once before, back in high school while playing tackle football in the school gym.

"I was blindside tackled by a kid who was thrown out of three other high schools," said Prince.

That injury also required more than average medical attention. A neurosurgeon had to reattach the tendon to the nerve. This time, Edgar Prince tracked down the same surgeon, who agreed to meet the Princes at the hospital early Monday morning to do it all over again. But there was a hitch: Erik had to be back in Annapolis by Tuesday morning. The Navy was strict about its rules. Edgar Prince called for the company jet.

Prince had the surgery on Monday morning and recovered just briefly before leaving the hospital. On Tuesday morning, he was headed back to Annapolis, feeling confident that he wouldn't get into trouble. He had called ahead and explained what had happened.

Prince arrived in Annapolis on his father's jet thirty minutes late. As he recounts it, the officer of the day didn't show any sympathy for his ordeal, and Prince was written up for his tardiness. It was the last straw for a young man with little patience for rules that made no sense to him.

Shortly after that, Prince decided to leave the Naval Academy. He had already started looking for another school, and he settled quickly on the small conservative campus of Hillsdale College, in rural southern Michigan.

"I visited some other schools before breaking out of the academy," Prince recalled. "I really liked Hillsdale. I really liked their economics and business program." He also liked the school's flexibility. Hillsdale would admit him that year and accept most of his college credits earned at the Naval Academy.

For the young man who prided himself on his deep patriotism, quitting the Naval Academy seemed an astonishing decision. Yet it showed another side to Prince that his father fully understood and supported: a deep, gut-level individualism and sense of right and wrong. While the slight over his tardy return was a matter of rules and regulation, routine in military academies, Prince would have none of it.

Prince may have lost confidence in the academy, but he never lost sight of becoming a sailor, and he had set his sights on getting back into the Navy. He used his time at Hillsdale to build up his resumé for the task at hand. While attending classes, Prince volunteered at the local fire department, where he eventually became an emergency medical technician.

"I was the first guy from my college to do that, and it was great," recalled Prince. "I wore a radio to class and did my training at night and was a fully qualified, paid firefighter."

It didn't pay much, but he wasn't doing it for the money.

"I thought it was a great way to serve and to get to know the guys," said Prince. "It was a great leadership experience because I was a junior guy and earning the confidence of a guy that was a butcher, a guy that was a mechanic; there was a cross section of guys."

Prince turned his back on the Greek fraternity system at Hillsdale and the parties that came with them. He wanted to be sure that if and when the call came to fight a fire, he would be sober and ready to take it on. The thought of being out of control had no appeal to him.

What did appeal to him was Austrian economics. Only at Hillsdale would such a major exist. In 1871 Carl Menger published *Principles of Economics*. He would go on to become the founder of the Austrian school. Menger believed that the science of human action was built on deductive logic. Others built on his writings. In 1912 Ludwig von Mises published *The Theory of Money and Credit*, still considered one of the great texts in free market liberalism. Von Mises heralded the contributions of business to society and presented a strong opposition to taxes and government regulations that would curb enterprise. Hillsdale, with its intense devotion to conservative values, offered an economics major in von Mises's name. In Hillsdale classrooms Prince would gain a new appreciation of the interrelationship between markets and politics and a near-religious belief that markets were almost always adversely affected by politics.

"I'm a very free market guy. I'm not a huge believer that government provides a whole lot of solutions," said Prince. "Some think that government can solve society's problems. I tend to think private charities and private organizations are better solutions."

Prince also credited a big part of his views on politics and the marketplace to the time he spent in Washington. He managed to land a highly coveted internship in the White House of President George H. W. Bush, only to find that just like the Naval Academy, the experience wasn't what he expected.

As a White House intern, Prince made photocopies and helped set up meetings for various constituent groups. But he saw things he didn't like. One thing that bothered him: homosexual groups were invited into the White House. He also noticed the enormous size of the federal bureaucracy—more evidence of wasteful government, he thought.

"Having that White House internship responsibility and badges, I walked around some of these other cavernous federal agencies, and you want to talk about depressing? Walk through HHS [Health and Human Services] or HUD [Housing and Urban Development] or Commerce, you name it. Leviathan realized."

Though Prince says he never met the president, he clearly developed opinions about the way Bush Sr. was running the White House. He thought the elder Bush was abandoning conservative principles.

Prince connected more closely with old family friend Chuck Colson during his time in Washington. The two had dinner while Prince was interning at the White House. A much more direct mentor relationship was forming, one that would grow stronger with time.

FROM THE MOMENT Prince left the Naval Academy, he focused his efforts on finding a way to get back into the Navy. His idea was to apply for the Sea, Air, and Land Special Operations Forces, better known as the SEALs. He wanted to belong to the elite brotherhood he considered the best of the best.

An encounter at a dinner he attended one evening offered a rare opportunity to help make that happen. "I sat down at this table, and to my left was a guy with two hearing aids who could hardly hear anything, so I started talking to the guy on my right," recalled Prince. "I said, 'I'm in college, I'm doing an internship, and I really want to go to OCS [Officer Candidate School], and I really want to be a SEAL,' and that was before I knew anything about this guy. And he said, 'That's funny; I just retired as a SEAL, and I was a captain and commander of BUD/S [Basic Underwater Demolition/SEAL].'" Prince befriended the retired captain, who later introduced him to some serving SEALs, giving Prince the opportunity to ask questions and make sure it was a lifestyle he wanted. The encounter only solidified his determination to join them. It was a challenge, and if there was anything the young Prince loved, it was a challenge.

Another chance meeting gave him a glimmer of hope about Washington politics. Out one night with some friends from the Hill, Prince met conservative Republican Congressman Dana Rohrabacher at a bowling alley.

"I told him I was interning at the White House, and I didn't really like how it was going, and he said, 'Hey, come intern in my office,'" Prince recalled. It was the beginning of a relationship that would last well beyond the five-month internship.

"He's a very impressive young man," said Rohrabacher. "He's physically and mentally and in many other ways a very impressive person."

Rohrabacher said he didn't know at the time that Prince's parents were "gazillionaires," but he did know that Prince was a "conservative activist."

Prince spent his time in Rohrabacher's office focusing on foreign policy issues. It seemed the perfect place and time for someone with such intense interest in the military. The United States was in the middle of the first Gulf War.

Iraq had invaded Kuwait in August 1990. By January 1991, about the time Prince began interning for Rohrabacher, there were over a half million allied troops in the gulf region, mostly at the Saudi border, preparing to push Saddam Hussein's troops back to Baghdad. By mid-January, the allied forces had begun a devastating bombing campaign in Baghdad, and by the end of February, with Iraqi forces out of Kuwait, President Bush ordered a cease-fire. In one of the most controversial points of the short-lived war, Iraqi troops were allowed to slip back into southern Iraq. Saddam was left in power.

Erik Prince was learning to look critically at government decision making, and he was finding other like-minded people with whom he could talk politics. Paul Behrends, a former Marine, had met Congressman Rohrabacher while he was stationed at Special Operations Command Europe in Stuttgart, Germany. Rohrabacher was a speechwriter for President Ronald Reagan back then. The two hit it off, and Rohrabacher offered him a job. Behrends remembers working with the intern intensely interested in what was happening in the world.

"I was just very impressed that he was a thinking person," remembered Behrends. "He wouldn't listen to other people and kind of regurgitate the prepackaged ideas of someone else. He did his own analysis and his own thinking."

Prince made a similar impression on Rohrabacher, who would remain a good friend and staunch defender of Prince.

"It's pretty much no nonsense with Erik," said Rohrabacher. "He's not like one of the guys who I'd think would be out just drinking and joking around; he really is a pretty serious person."

Rohrabacher would help foster the bonds of friendship between Behrends and Prince by sending the two on research trips together. One of their first visits was to Croatia and Slovenia, both on the cusp of civil war, both ready to declare independence from Yugoslavia.

"It was like the dawn of a serious conflict," said Behrends. "There was a lot of tension in the air, and there was not a lot of attention about what was going on in Croatia in official Washington. So even though we were extremely junior people, we met with extremely senior officials."

The war that soon broke out would be noted for its brutality and ethnic hatred. Prince paid close attention to the military posturing he saw.

"I could have told you," said Prince, "even my novice impression, the guards, the weapons, the readiness that Slovenia had; you could tell they were ready to defend that country. Croatia wasn't as organized. The material readiness was markedly different in Slovenia than it was in Croatia."

The trip made a lasting impression on both men. Another trip, in early spring of 1991, made perhaps an even greater impression.

A short-lived civil war in Nicaragua in the late 1970s had brought Marxist Sandinista guerrillas to power under Daniel Ortega. Throughout much of the 1980s, the United States sponsored anti-Sandinista rebels known as the Contras.

The years of conflict had seen the killing of tens of thousands of people and had had a devastating effect on the economy. In 1990 Ortega was finally swept from office in free elections. Now, a year later, Congressman Rohrabacher sent Prince and Behrends to pave the way for his own visit.

There were reports of mass graves in the Nicaraguan countryside. Several investigations were under way. The intern and the former Marine headed off to search for evidence of past atrocities.

"We were actually going out in the jungle areas where the Sandinistas had murdered large numbers of people," recalled Rohrabacher. "He [Prince] volunteered to go down and make sure we were digging in the right location and basically started digging up the graves before we got there so we knew we weren't wasting our time."

Both Prince and Behrends described the experience as "surreal." They solicited the help of a local man, who led them to a place in the countryside.

"We took some samples, and sure enough, there were a whole lot of human remains. Some skulls had been shattered, and the people's arms had been tied behind their backs," Prince remembered.

It was a close-up lesson in cruelty and political atrocities hauntingly familiar to Prince after his family's visit to the former concentration camp at Dachau. While he was witnessing history in the making, Prince had to cut his trip short. He left his team in Nicaragua before their work was done for a pressing personal matter: he was getting married.

Prince met Joan Nicole Keating on a blind date while enrolled at the Naval Academy. She was the sister of a good friend and fellow cadet. The two wed in mid-April and embarked on an unconventional honeymoon that he dubbed the "Baltic Liberation Tour."

"Most people who have been to Europe have been to London, Paris, Berlin, but not too many to Romania," said Prince. "We went to Latvia, Lithuania, Estonia, which was actually still occupied by the Russians, by the Soviets." The two spent their first days as a married couple traveling through Poland, East Germany, Czechoslovakia, Hungary, Romania, Serbia, Bosnia, and Croatia.

AFTER HIS HONEYMOON and subsequent graduation from Hillsdale, Prince concentrated his focus again on the SEALs. There were no more spots available at Officer Candidate School, and the idea of waiting another year to enroll was more than he could stand, so he called up the captain he had met at that dinner months earlier.

"I said, 'Look, Captain, I can't really put my life on hold for another year. I gotta do this, you know? What can I do?'" recalled Prince. The captain made a few phone calls, and, as Prince put it, "The rest was history."

A few days after his last final exam at Hillsdale, Prince packed up and headed to Officer Candidate School. He was so anxious to get there and finish something he had started years earlier that he didn't even attend his own graduation.

"I left the Naval Academy because I didn't like it, and I hated to leave something and not finish it, so I was gonna finish this one way or the other, come hell or high water."

CHAPTER 2

Hell and High Water

IN 1962 President John F. Kennedy had a vision: he believed that the nature of warfare was changing and that conventional wars with large numbers of troops wouldn't suffice for the changing nature of the threats the country faced. Smaller, specially trained units would be vital to the nation's defense. During World War II, underwater demolition teams had been used successfully to clear potential battlefields ahead of the arrival of large numbers of troops. Building on that concept, Kennedy established the Navy SEALs, an elite maritime fighting body composed of the best-trained, physically and mentally toughest men the Navy could find. The SEALs took their name from the go-anywhere theaters of Sea, Air, and Land. Their missions would be clandestine.

The challenge of becoming a Navy SEAL is legendary. Candidates are pushed to physical and mental limits they scarcely imagined. Many of them can't handle it. In any given class, barely one-third of the candidates make it through. There are no real indicators of which candidates will succeed and which won't.

Enlisted men train alongside officers; men of intense physical conditioning train with men who may appear slight; and men who may already have a few years of experience train with men who have no military experience at all. Trainers will tell you there is generally only one trait that Navy SEALs share: sheer determination.

Despite Prince's impatience with many of the time-honored traditions of the Naval Academy, he was committed to becoming a SEAL. Yet he would become an officer first.

The Navy's Officer Candidate School is located near Rhode Island's Narragansett Bay, an area rich in American history. Around the time of the Revolutionary War, the British had used it as a base of operations to control what moved in and out of the territories. When an American-friendly French fleet approached, however, a British general gave the order to abandon the bay. Many historians credit it as a pivotal loss of advantage for the British and a turning point in the war.

ONE OF PRINCE'S FELLOW officer candidates, Bill Mathews, had already gone to college and then law school to become an attorney when he realized the law really wasn't where his heart was. "I didn't want to be an old, fat, stodgy lawyer," recalled Mathews. "My roommate from college had actually dropped out and gone into the Navy and became a SEAL, and he told me fabulous stories about how great it was to be a frogman." Mathews was just twenty-five years old when he got in his car one day and started driving.

"I ended up driving from Bloomington, Indiana, to Indianapolis, not knowing where I was going when I got in the car. I ended up at the naval recruiting depot," Mathews recalled. "I loved to be outside, I loved to hike and swim. I was a swimmer in college, and so being in the water was something I got a lot of enjoyment out of. I kept wondering how in the heck can you make a living camping and swimming and doing all of these things I liked to do. The only thing that fit the bill was being a SEAL."

Mathews was so eager to get on with the next phase of his life that he showed up at OCS in Newport, Rhode Island, days before classes were to start. "Somebody told me to go find a retired master chief out at the school's swimming pool, so I drove out there to find him," said Mathews. He found the master chief, but he wasn't the only eager young candidate to do so. Erik Prince was also at the pool. "He was an average guy," recalls Mathews. "A great big, strong, strapping guy, but he was average, very, very average."

The two struck up a conversation. Mathews thought Prince was just another candidate; he had no idea that he hailed from a family of enormous wealth and privilege. "He had an old, crappy brown Jeep. I remember it because it was parked next to mine, and I had a brand-new black Jeep that I was very proud of," said Mathews. As far as he knew, Prince was an unassuming guy from a modest background.

The twelve-week officer candidate course is designed to provide its students with a working knowledge of the Navy, with particular emphasis on physical training, military knowledge, and academic courses. Prince didn't find the tasks all that tough. The hardest transition for him would be going from the freedoms of college life to the rigors of a military one. "The biggest challenge is having somebody else tell you what to do," said Prince. "What time you had to be there, what time you had to get up, what time you had to go to bed, what to wear that day, living under someone else's direct control." Erik Prince belonged to the U.S. military now, and this time, he was determined to succeed in what he set out to do: to become part of the military brotherhood. These first twelve weeks were just a warm-up.

Up next: Basic Underwater Demolition/SEAL training. Candidates are drawn from all over the Navy, with only a limited number of slots reserved for officers. Prince and Mathews both landed spots.

BUD/S candidates spend six months at the Naval Special Warfare Training Center in Coronado, California. After a five-week initial indoctrination, the training is divided into three phases that cover basic conditioning, diving, and land warfare. Candidates are tested to their limits. It's a grueling experience, during which many of the candidates form intense bonds.

One of the first people Prince met in Coronado was Jeff Gibson. To get through college, Gibson had joined the military's Reserve Officers' Training Corp (ROTC) because it provided money for an education while introducing students to the military life. Gibson originally intended to become a pilot. With good eyesight and good grades, he was confident in his chances of qualifying for flight school.

During the summers between his college years, Gibson kept busy. He went to sea for four weeks, spent time with aviation experts, spent a week with the Marines, spent a week on a submarine, and then, during the summer between his junior and senior years, served time on a ship in San Diego. One of Gibson's shipmates asked if he wanted to go with him to Coronado to check out the SEALs. Gibson had never even heard of them. "I seriously thought that he was talking about marine mammals. And I go, 'OK, cool.' So we go over there, and I'm asking, 'So, where are these seals at?'" recalled Gibson. "Then it kind of dawned on me."

Gibson's buddy had a friend who gave them a tour of BUD/S and the SEAL training grounds. It was enough to make Gibson change his plans: pilots were cool, but SEALs were much cooler. He applied but didn't get a spot. He took the next best thing: training as a

Navy diver. He completed dive school and was assigned to a ship that turned out to be a support ship for SEALs training.

"For two years," said Gibson, "I'd have all these SEALs come onboard and launch their boats and do submarine operations, and I was just like, 'Oh my gosh, I've got to get back there.'" He did, and that's where he met Prince and Mathews.

On the first day of training, more than 120 men gathered on the California beach. Many of the candidates couldn't help but look around on that first day, wondering who would still be there at the end. "I remember just sitting there going, 'Holy crap. That guy, he looks like he's in shape; that guy, he's not gonna make it,'" said Gibson. "It turns out the guy I thought wouldn't make it, he was kinda dumpy and unkempt, you know, he turned out to be one of the best guys in our class, and then the guy who was all in shape and cut up, he was one of the first to quit." By the time the course concluded, only thirty-four of them would remain.

Like Gibson, Chris Burgess also came up through the Navy's ROTC program. After spending two years navigating ships in the naval fleet, he earned a slot in the BUD/S program. From the very beginning, the men would form bonds that would last well beyond any of their naval careers. Even on the first day of training, when the men earned a little extra attention from the instructors, their personalities and esprit de corps emerged together.

"Bill got the class into trouble," said Burgess. The class was given rules: "to stand in the surf and get cold." That's when Mathews made a fateful decision. "'Well, we're in the surf; they can't do anything to us, so let's do a conga line,'" Burgess remembered Mathews saying. "So he gets the guys around him to do a conga line. The instructors got incredibly mad, saying, 'OK, fine, you think that's funny? You're gonna stay in there a long time.'"

The instructors singled out Prince and Mathews and ordered

them to play "beached whale." It was a punishment in which both men were ordered to lie on their stomachs in the sand with the waves crashing up over their heads as they pretended to wiggle in and out of the water. They had to take water into their mouths and spit it out, much like a whale would do. Prince found it a humbling experience.

"The waves are washing up on the shore and right over your head, and when they're out is when you breathe," recalled Prince. "You lie there, and every orifice of your body and pants and everything else gets filled with sand. It's miserable."

Because Prince was married, he was among the few BUD/S candidates allowed to live off base. He and Joan settled into a condo just down the beach from where Prince and his buddies tested their physical and mental limits on a daily basis. Joan would often cook for the hungry crew, and the men would share stories around the hot tub. Erik and Joan's place became known as "Hotel Tango."

Prince's marriage at a very young age wasn't the only thing that set him apart from the other guys. He was also deeply religious and quite open about sharing his opinions. Gibson was a Catholic and had fallen in love with a woman who didn't share his faith. He asked Prince for advice on how to teach his fiancée about the Catholic Church and its history. "My wife would ask me a lot of questions about faith and why do you guys do this and why do you do that, and I couldn't answer her, but Erik could," said Gibson. Shortly after that conversation, Erik and Joan invited Gibson and his fiancée to dinner, and they talked a lot about faith and the church. Erik's religion had been an intimate part of his upbringing, and he had continued to practice his deep faith even after leaving his parents' home and starting a new family of his own. Part of that faith was making sure that others had the answers they needed to find God in their own lives.

Phase 1 of BUD/S training is said to be the hardest. It includes eight weeks of intense conditioning—running, swimming, and physical drills—that allow the instructors the opportunity to see the candidates' strengths and mental toughness. The infamous "Hell Week" falls in this first phase of training. Those who have been through it will tell you it is exactly that: hell. As many as two-thirds of BUD/S candidates can find the physical and mental demands too much and call it quits during the week that begins with the pounding reverberations of an M-60 machine gun. Trainees are in constant motion for the next five and a half days, and sleep deprivation is a real concern.

Some say the fear of failure keeps them going. Others, like Mathews, can't afford to think about the possibility. Dropping out requires ringing a giant brass bell, a public proclamation of failure.

"If you're gonna be a SEAL, you can't really think about failure as an option," said Mathews. "The guys who would entertain what it might be like to quit all ended up quitting, so, in particular with BUD/S, even more than with Officer Candidate School, if you got there with that thought in your head, you were in trouble."

Traditionally, when Hell Week comes to an end, candidates are usually more confident for having made it past one of the toughest tests they may ever face. They've also learned to rely on each other.

Phase 2 of BUD/S training is the dive phase: eight weeks of underwater drills and learning everything there is to know about dive operations. It can be a challenge both academically and physically, as candidates learn what can happen to the human body on a deep sea dive.

Mathews, already infamous for masterminding the conga line, discovered how much of a friend Prince could be during a swim. The men were expected to wear life vests equipped with CO_2 cartridges, so that if they ran into a problem, they could pull a toggle and the vest would inflate to keep the swimmer afloat. The men lined up for inspection by the instructors, and Mathews realized he had a problem.

"I showed up for the swim without my CO_2 cartridge," said Mathews. "Mind you, the CO_2 cartridge is brass, and it has to be shiny and polished and no fingerprints on it. It has to be pristine before you go jump in the ocean with it. Erik gave me his good one and took an old cruddy one that wasn't polished. He ended up getting in trouble and they wrote him up and gave him a safety violation. It was the only one he'd ever gotten in the Navy."

Prince's fellow BUD/S candidates were already coming to respect him, even though he was younger than many of them. "There was a class on the M-16 [machine gun], and I'd never picked up a gun before I got in the Navy," recalled Mathews. "It's all new stuff to me. As we walk out, Erik starts describing the difference in mechanical function between the M-16 and the Uzi and the M-60, along with the corporate history of the Colt Manufacturing Company." At first, Mathews thought Prince might just be a gun nut. He soon realized that Prince was a walking encyclopedia of all things that captured his attention.

Prince made the effort to balance his married life with his military one, though it sometimes wasn't easy. Many of the guys would go for a drink after a hard day, and while Prince would sometimes join them, he rarely made an evening out of it, usually leaving before any of the others so he could get home. When Prince was there, the mood was different. "If we'd go out, he'd have maybe, like, one or two beers and then go. He was just really responsible," said Gibson. "If he was there, I'd be like, 'Oh, shit, Erik, I guess we can't get too crazy.'"

"We emptied our bank accounts and drank entirely too much beer, and Erik didn't, and at the time I probably perceived him as being a little stiff," remembered Mathews. "But you know, he was in uniform; he shouldn't have been drinking. Erik typically does what's right."

For Prince, the balance between being a military man and a married one wasn't easy. "It was a two-edged sword because I got to go home at night, but it also gave me all the other domestic challenges or things to worry about, things like a toilet that was backed up or house stuff that you had to fix," he said. "Compared to the guys that lived on base, they had a room and a bathroom and a little efficiency kitchen, and that was all they had to worry about. They didn't have a spouse. What do wives want to do at the end of the day? They want to talk about how your day was. I didn't want to talk about how my day was; it was miserable. I just wanted to get through it and get on to the next day."

Joan, too, strove for normalcy. She had a job as a teacher at a local school and befriended a lot of people in their small community. She would often invite them over to socialize, something that also didn't always work out well.

"I just remember being tired all the time," said Prince, "and she'd make these great dinners, invite people over, and I'd just be falling asleep over my food at night. I'd have to excuse myself because I'd have to get up and sharpen my knife or polish my CO_2 cartridge or polish my boots."

At the end of phase 2, Prince's fatigue got the better of him.

It was standard for candidates to run through obstacle courses as part of their training. Many courses were equipped with safety nets on the high-rise portions in the event of a fall, but one was not. Prince had already tackled the course the day before. This time, he was descending a long diagonal rope and holding it higher than he should have been to keep a firm balance. He didn't know the guy below him on the same rope was about to jump off, creating a whip effect. Prince tried to keep his grip but couldn't, and fell forty feet to the ground. He didn't get up.

"My hip got canted and kind of locked," remembered Prince, "and my left leg was about two inches shorter than my right leg." A doctor took a look at Prince's injuries, twisted him into a position, pressed all of his own body weight onto Prince, and something popped. Apparently, he'd had a dislocated hip. It seemed to do the trick, and Prince moved on to the final phase of training at San Clemente Island, California. His buddies were astonished.

"Erik was on the plane and made it out to San Clemente Island because he was bound and determined not to get left behind," recalled Mathews. It meant that Erik could complete training with his class and wouldn't have to be "rolled back" to finish with another class while he tended to his injuries.

Phase 3 of BUD/S training involved nine weeks of land warfare training. Candidates learned demolition, reconnaissance, and land warfare. They also developed skills for clearing beach obstacles, something that the early underwater demolition teams did in World War II before beach landings.

While Prince was becoming more skilled with the drills and intense training, he chafed at the chain of command. In one warfare drill, Gibson and Prince were in the same platoon; Gibson was in charge, and Prince was his assistant officer. The team had just one day to plan and practice a night operation in which another platoon was supposed to ambush them.

"They ended up taking one of our guys and acting like they had killed him. They picked Erik," recounted Gibson. "They said, 'OK, Erik, you're down,' and he was all pissed off. 'Why do I gotta be down? Why can't I be the assaulter?'" He hated not being in the action.

Despite the frustration, the fatigue of six months of intense training, and his forty-foot fall, Prince graduated from BUD/S with his three friends. Only thirty-three others in SEAL class 188 made the cut. Prince considers his graduation day one of the best of his life. He had finally gotten his shot, and he had succeeded.

But the successful completion of BUD/S is still not enough to earn the Navy trident—the gold eagle and trident emblem that is the pride of SEAL teams. Those who graduate from BUD/S are sent off for six months of additional training. SEAL Qualification Training (SQT) covers such basic skills as static line and free fall tactical air operations (TACAIR), land warfare, tactical medicine, and close quarter combat. Prince successfully completed his SEAL training and earned his Navy trident. He was a Navy SEAL.

SEAL OPERATIONS are largely covert, and there are only eight known SEAL teams operating today. Erik Prince was assigned to SEAL Team 8. A team is made up of ten platoons, each with sixteen SEALs, two of them officers, the rest enlisted. Platoons are further divided into two squads of eight, which in turn comprise two fire teams of four men, two pairs of swim buddies. Prince was an officer, which meant he was personally in charge of the enlisted men assigned to him.

His career as a SEAL would last only two years. It would take him to Haiti, Bosnia, and the Middle East, some of the flash points of the Clinton years.

Signs of instability were beginning to simmer in Haiti, one of the poorest countries in the Western Hemisphere. The country was of enormous strategic importance to the United States, which had a long history of intervention in Haiti. It had occupied the Caribbean nation from 1915 to 1934, keeping open the option to develop a naval base. Haiti was a pawn that would not be sacrificed.

The United States had hoped that the country was turning to democracy in December 1990 when Jean-Bertrand Aristide won Haiti's first free election. Much to the dismay of Washington, however, Aristide was ousted by a military coup in 1991. In response, the United States launched a diplomatic mission that lasted more than three years, trying to return Aristide to power.

In September 1994, President Bill Clinton sent troops to Haiti to maintain order. The SEALs played a key part in the operation, clearing the way for troops by making their way onshore and securing the airport on the outskirts of Port-au-Prince. It was Prince's first deployment. He and his team were ready. "You've spent so much time with them," said Prince, "you could spot them in a dark field at night by how they walk."

It was just a month later that Aristide was restored to power. Prince would go on to serve deployments in Bosnia and the Middle East as well, but in a post–cold war world, he would spend much of his time away from his wife, either onboard an aircraft carrier or at one of the scattered training facilities the Navy used across the United States for weapons training. While Prince saw no actual combat, he did see a drawdown on the training side that concerned him. He poured his frustration into a letter home to Joan, outlining his ardent wish for a facility where Special Operations Forces teams could train together and go home to their families at night. Being away from home was hell on a young family, especially with Joan expecting the couple's first child.

By the time Joan gave birth to a healthy baby girl, Prince was feeling the demands of the military pulling him in a frustrating direction. He had increasing responsibilities at home, and ultimately he would be forced to choose how to better serve both his country and his family. Adding to the stress, his daughter Sophia's christening in Michigan just a few months later would be the very last time Prince would see his father alive.

"I'll never forget saying good-bye to him; there was something about it. I always gave my dad a kiss goodbye," recalled Prince. "That day I think I kissed him good-bye three or four times, and I said, 'Dad, I love you, I miss you, and I can't wait to see you again,' and that was it." On the morning of March 2, 1995, sixty-three-year-old Edgar Prince left the executive dining room at work. He got into the elevator for the ride up to his office, but by the time the doors opened, he was lying on the floor. He had suffered a massive heart attack.

News traveled quickly in the small town of Holland. Many of the residents had worked for Edgar Prince for years. Yet the news failed to immediately reach the one person who most needed to know. Erik's mother, Elsa, was at lunch with college friends as employees were desperately trying to reach her.

"Ed knew where I was, the fellow who helps us around our house knew where I was, but nobody else knew where I was," recalled Elsa. "In the meantime, they had called our other children."

Erik was with his SEAL team when he got the phone call
from one of his father's friends and business advisers. "I had an
urgent message to call him. He was crying on the phone, and he
said, 'Erik, your dad's had a heart attack, and it doesn't look good.'
But he wouldn't say if he was dead or not, just that they were
working on him."

Erik called his wife and told her to pack a bag, and not to forget
his uniform; if there was a funeral, he would need it. Company
employees arranged for a plane to pick the couple up. When they
arrived at the airport in Michigan, a friend of Edgar Prince's was
waiting for them. As Prince remembered, "We got off the plane,
and he said, 'Erik, your dad's gone.'"

It wasn't just a profound shock; it was a life-changing one.
"There was all of a sudden a change of his focus in life," said
Mathews. "Instead of focusing on career and the Navy, which I
know he loved dearly, he shifted focus because he had responsibilities at home."

About three weeks after his father died, Erik was in the
Nevada desert with his SEAL platoon. Their training ended on
Friday, and a Navy flight was scheduled to pick them up the following Monday. Prince saw a better use for his time and asked
his task unit commander if he could call for a company jet to pick
him up. He needed to work through some business issues with
his mother.

Edgar Prince sat atop a billion-dollar empire when he died. In
just three decades, he had grown a $160,000 initial investment
into an automotive company with five thousand employees and
eight manufacturing plants. The company was reporting revenues
of more than $500 million. Erik had always entertained the idea
of one day returning to work for his father, but he wasn't ready
to tackle the family business without him. With no heir apparent

inside the company, Elsa and her children decided to sell. Within months, they had a suitor in Johnson Controls, which advertised itself as the world's largest seat-system supplier. The Milwaukee-based company that had facilities in eighteen countries offered $1.35 billion in cash. The deal was soon done.

It was the kind of money that makes some people adopt a life of leisure, but not Erik Prince. He knew he would always have an enormous safety net. Yet he refused to sit back and relax. If anything, the sudden inheritance offered a whole new world of opportunity.

KEN VIERA was a training officer for SEAL Team 8 in Little Creek, Virginia, in 1995 when he met Erik Prince. "He was just another young, strapping, bright-eyed officer wanting to do great things within the SEAL community," recalled Viera. "I do remember he was very patriotic."

Viera didn't pay particular attention to Prince in the early days, seeing him as another eager young officer like the others, until he caught wind of conversations Prince had with one of Viera's firearms instructors, Al Clark, about starting a new training facility. The SEALS relied on training facilities for everything from shooting practice, to demolitions, to diving, to a whole menu of tactical capabilities. Since the mid-1980s, SEAL teams had been using a facility in Tennessee that Viera found adequate but not ideal. The location made little sense, and SEAL teams often found themselves competing for range time with other trainees. For years, Viera had heard talk within the naval community of searching for a more convenient place to train. "It was beer talk," said Viera. "Converting that beer talk into action is a large step." Now, Prince was talking about doing something very real.

Clark had a passion for firearms. Prince's vision, and his new financial means, were irresistible. Viera, too, was dying to improve SEAL training. "We were the best of the best in the organization," said Viera, "and we don't even have a great training facility. It was almost criminal."

Viera began asking around about what Prince had in mind. Finally, one afternoon, he called Prince into his office. Viera already had twenty-four years of service under his belt and liked the idea of doing something different.

"I asked Erik to pop in one day," said Viera. "We sat down, and I mentioned to him that I'd heard he and Al Clark were working on an idea." Prince explained the basic concept. The conversation ended with an offer. "I said, 'Hey, Erik, if you're interested and things line up, consider my name as a participant in helping you guys kick this thing off,'" remembered Viera.

There was one other acquaintance from Prince's brief stint in the SEALs who would later prove to become a driving force of Blackwater, though he hardly seemed important at first. One of Prince's duties as a young officer was to conduct investigations, and he was assigned to investigate a fight involving a young SEAL who had allegedly bitten the ear off another young man in a bar fight over a woman. The SEAL under investigation was assigned to a facility run by Gary Jackson.

"I came up, and I said I need to see Petty Officer so-and-so, and he showed me the way," said Prince. "I interviewed him and came back and interviewed Gary. I just remember him to be a very high-energy, likable guy." Jackson recounted the first meeting with slightly less enthusiasm. Ten years his junior, Prince was just another young officer doing his job, or so he thought at the time. Little did either of them know that they would eventually become inseparable as the owner and president of Blackwater.

PRINCE HAS ALWAYS LIVED a full life, rushing forward at top speed. As he made serious plans to leave the Navy and start a new venture, one year after the death of his father, he was blindsided—but hardly deterred—by terrible news at home. Joan was well into her pregnancy with the couple's second child. Then, one day, she felt a lump in her breast. It was big enough that she made an appointment with her doctors, who didn't want to wait for the baby's natural arrival before addressing the potential cancer. Doctors advised Joan and Erik to induce labor early so that they could get a better look at the lump and recommend treatment. The Princes were deeply concerned about what effect inducing early might have on the baby, but they did it anyway. Joan gave birth to the couple's second child, their first son, Christian, but it wasn't an ideal birth.

"He had some trouble for the first eight or nine days; it was exactly what we told them we didn't want to happen. We had been willing to wait a few more weeks until he was fully developed, so his lungs were good, but he came out early and spent over a week in the intensive care unit," recalled Prince. Joan was twenty-nine years old. It was the spring of 1996. With their son out of danger, Joan focused on treating her cancer. She wasn't aware of any history of breast cancer in her family, but once she started looking closer, she found a few cousins and an aunt who had had it.

Prince had a tough decision to make. He had put in a request to extend his active duty time in the Navy because he loved being a SEAL, but he could scarcely afford to be away from home now. It was too much to handle. "With my dad having passed away, and then Joan had cancer, there were two straws that broke the camel's back, so I got out."

Erik and Joan focused on learning what they could about the disease threatening to tear their family apart. The couple flew to Europe, where there were treatments being given to cancer patients that weren't yet accepted in the United States. When Joan appeared to go into remission, they thought they had it beat, at least for a while. Erik retired as a Navy SEAL and launched himself into a startup business that would allow him to spend more time at home: he would focus on providing the training facilities he had wanted during his SEAL career.

CHAPTER 3

The Blackwater Project

KEN VIERA was an early convert to Prince's cause. He promptly submitted his retirement papers and signed on full-time to help get the venture off the ground. It was a dream come true for the career serviceman interested in a new adventure.

Al Clark also left the Navy SEALS, and the men set up shop in an office in Virginia Beach. The company that still had no name was looking to locate near the U.S. Navy in Norfolk, Virginia. Naval Station Norfolk was abuzz with military activity, servicing aircraft and ships in the naval fleet; it was also the headquarters for both the naval base and air station, and an added bonus: the Navy SEALs operated out of the Little Creek Naval Amphibious Base.

The men knew they needed to be close to Norfolk to attract clients. Clark and Prince began a massive search for property and found more than 3,000 acres just forty-eight miles away in Moyock, North Carolina. It was in the middle of bear country. The location was far from prying eyes, yet still within an hour's drive from the Navy hub. They wanted to make it easy for the Navy to do business with them.

"It changes some of the orders as far as people being on per diem and not going on per diem," recounted Viera. "Being under fifty miles, it's just a day trip."

Prince was anticipating growth and looking for lots of land. He and the others were committed to the idea of designing and building the new facility based on military specs for outdoor complexes. If it would all go the way he imagined, he would need to buy enough land so that he could expand easily.

"Erik bought capacity right up front," said Viera, "so you know it was a bold move. We didn't know that 2001 would happen and 9/11. But the move played itself out well."

Coming up with a name for the company was next on the list. Someone suggested Blackwater, as it described the land itself—anywhere in that region there was thick, dark, swampy water running just below the surface of the ground. The company's logo, in a nod to the local fauna, would be a bear paw print. As work began to clear the land, Viera invited another SEAL to come and take a look at the project.

Ken Viera and Gary Jackson had been personal and professional friends for years. Though they never served at any one command together, they had kept in touch as warrant officers. They shared a great deal of mutual respect. Jackson visited the property while the land was still being cleared. Viera laid out the vision. Jackson was convinced the idea would work. His drive and determination were among the attributes Viera had long admired.

Jackson, a SEAL officer who had once been in charge of a counterdrug platoon in the Caribbean, had long toyed with business aspirations. He had begun dabbling in writing Web pages in the late 1990s. Now, still in the Navy, he auditioned for the job. "I wrote a Web site for the company," recalled Jackson. "I mailed it to them on a three-and-a-half-inch disk."

While Jackson admitted the Web site wasn't very good, the effort was enough to get Prince's attention. He remembered their brief encounter from years before when Erik was investigating the ear-biting incident.

In January 1998, Jackson came home to Chesapeake, Virginia, to bury his father. Viera stopped by his house to talk about making Jackson's relationship with Blackwater more official. "I was trying to be really suave," said Jackson. "I said, 'Can I have twenty-four hours to think about this?'"

Jackson had already spent twenty-three years in the Navy. He was as high as he could go rank-wise. Like Viera, he was looking for a new challenge. He called the next day and accepted the job. "I was just over forty years old, and I was going to retire, and I was going to work six to eight hours a day helping them schedule, and I wasn't gonna do range time," Jackson told them. "I'd done all that, I had that T-shirt, and I wasn't gonna stand on the range for ten hours a day."

Jackson would instead rely on his computer skills to help build the company's Web site and lend a hand with scheduling and trying to help generate business. He imagined doing a little sales and working between six and seven hours a day in semiretirement. It didn't work out that way. "We started working extremely hard; it got into my blood very fast. I understood that we really were blessed and lucky guys, you know, the dozen people who were down here." It was such a small company at the time that even Jackson's wife came on board to help keep the books.

Al Clark also reached out to another fellow SEAL, Dale McClellan, who had trained with Prince and knew about his ideas to build the facility. "I could have one of these," McClellan remembered Prince saying as the two went through training drills at another facility months earlier. McClellan's response: "If you do, keep me in mind, because I want to come and work for you."

In the spring of 1998, their hard work was rewarded with the fledgling company's first paying customer: SEAL Team 5. Blackwater hadn't even officially opened yet. There was only one building, and the furniture hadn't arrived. It made for an anxious scene as the men awaited the arrival of the team. "I'll never forget the day they showed up," recalled Viera. "We gave them a quick brief. They left happy, and they were good customers beyond that."

It wasn't long afterward that Blackwater was ready to officially present itself to the law enforcement and Special Forces communities. An elaborate grand opening was staged with familiar faces from Prince's past, including California Representative Dana Rohrabacher. "Some other political types were invited," said Viera. "I gave a presentation that this was the future, this was the vision of providing the best training services for soldiers, sailors, airmen, and federal law enforcement."

At first, business was slow. The Navy already had a training program in place that had served it sufficiently for years. Shifting its attention toward Blackwater wouldn't happen quickly. The team did have some success with law enforcement, drawing an FBI SWAT team as an early client. They also opened up the property to civilians for firearms training as a stopgap measure to help raise some money and pay the bills. But training the private sector wasn't a sustainable business. Blackwater needed more government clients.

In the quest to find more business, the workdays expanded to between sixteen and seventeen hours, seven days a week. Weeks turned into months. Too often, not a single gun was fired on the property. Hourly workers were sent home early, and Jackson felt the pressure to pull out the stops. "I don't think the spam laws were in effect," said Jackson. "I was sending literally tens of thousands of e-mails. I got kicked out of the NRA show for guerrilla marketing down in Charlotte. It was just crazy."

Jackson's restless charisma found a new outlet in his salesmanship. He and the team drove thousands of miles to gun shows and trade shows. They made phone calls, sent e-mails— whatever would get people's attention. "I used to carry pockets full of these Blackwater magnets, and I would put them up in bathrooms [at trade shows], and I'd take the escalator, and I'd put them on the metal walls all the way up the escalator. It was a continuous obsession just to get the word out there, get Blackwater out there," he said.

In the end, two things saved the company, and neither of them had anything to do with gun shows or magnets. One was flexibility—a talent for adapting to a changing world. The other concerned exactly *how* the world was changing.

ON FRIDAY, AUGUST 7, 1998, at 10:34 in the morning, the streets of Nairobi, Kenya, were bustling with people going about their usual routines. It took less than a minute to turn the city upside down. A bomb ripped through an area outside the U.S. embassy, blowing apart a nearby structure. Within seconds, the scene turned from routine to one of blood and carnage. Body limbs were strewn everywhere, among a mass of twisted metal and broken concrete.

Within moments, another bomb exploded in a parking lot near the U.S. embassy in Dar es Salaam, Tanzania, over 400 miles away. Both buildings were considered "soft targets." They were lightly guarded, without much of a safety perimeter. The devastation was horrendous: 224 people were dead, among them 12 Americans. While there was no immediate claim of responsibility, U.S. intelligence agencies believed a group that called itself al-Qaeda was behind the carnage.

The FBI's response to the KENBOMB and TANBOMB attacks, as they became known among investigators, was the largest to date in the bureau's history. Some 900 special agents and employees were dispatched to Africa to recover evidence and track down those behind the attacks. Among those sent to investigate was Special Agent Ricky Chambers. Chambers had served six years in the Sacramento field office, had investigated child kidnapping cases, serial bank robberies, and white-collar crime, and had worked with the FBI's hostage rescue team in Quantico, Virginia. He'd never seen anything like what awaited him in Africa.

Chambers and his team of fellow investigators spent a month working alongside local police to uncover clues. Focusing on al-Qaeda led them to its leader, Osama bin Laden. Later that year, bin Laden was indicted in absentia for the bombings. A $5 million bounty was put on his head. Osama bin Laden was now the FBI's most wanted man.

The bombings highlighted the bureau's need to expand its ability to respond to incidents overseas that involved Americans. Acts of terror required quick reaction, and the CIA wasn't accustomed to events on this scale. The bombings were the beginning of a major change within the bureau. Working with U.S. intelligence agencies to dismantle terrorist support structures would become the FBI's number one priority.

Later that month, in response to the attacks and the evidence of al-Qaeda's involvement, the United States launched Operation Infinite Reach, unleashing a barrage of cruise missiles on suspected terror-related sites in Afghanistan and Sudan. One of the missiles destroyed the al-Shifa Pharmaceutical Factory, which the U.S. government believed was manufacturing chemical weapons. Though the chairman of the company denied any such production was happening there, U.S. intelligence experts believed otherwise.

Secretary of State Madeleine Albright spoke of America's war against terrorists and their infrastructure as "the war of the future." It would be fought with smaller, precision strikes against targets determined largely on the basis of intelligence information. It was a new kind of war that demanded new training, new targeting, and new technology.

IN 2001 Ricky Chambers became the FBI's assistant legal attaché in charge of training Kenya's investigative police unit while continuing the hunt for terror suspects. Chambers began working other cases as well, like the kidnapping of two American businessmen who had been lured to the country, then held for ransom.

"I was surprised with the amount of success I had working in a developing country," recalled Chambers. "Maybe being a black American got me a lot of mileage with the Kenyans, who have very rarely, if ever, met a black FBI agent." Chambers went by the nickname of C.T., which was short for Chocolate Thunder. He earned the name during a basketball game with colleagues in Quantico. It stuck, and he came to like it. Soon C.T. would realize he could use his skills and make a lot more doing it for Blackwater than he could at the bureau.

As the new war on terror unfolded gradually around the globe, Blackwater's focus was still largely at home. The company still hadn't turned a profit. Yet even local law enforcement groups understood they sorely needed a more adaptive and flexible force to be able to combat emerging terror threats.

On April 20, 1999, just before noon, seventeen-year-old Dylan Klebold and eighteen-year-old Eric Harris entered Columbine High School in Littleton, Colorado. Armed with guns and pipe bombs, the two students set off on a violent rampage, shooting almost everyone they encountered and showing no mercy for those too terrified to flee. The two had free rein over the hallways of Columbine for nearly an hour before they eventually killed themselves in the school library. The tragedy was laced with painful lessons for the law enforcement community. Police had not entered the school until forty minutes after the shooting began. The emergency response was so slow that some victims waited hours for medical attention.

The lessons were not lost on Prince, who saw a need for training in heavily populated environments. He introduced "R U Ready High School" to the Blackwater campus as a way for law enforcement to practice methods for securing schools and other locations under critical and immediate threat.

The company also focused on developing target systems that would fit the changing needs of law enforcement and Special Forces. Prince turned to Jim Dehart to develop more sophisticated, interactive targeting systems than the old-fashioned "aim for the black dot in the middle of the chest" breed. Dehart was a retired chief petty officer who had worked at the Naval Special Warfare Development Group for close to fifteen years. Prince called him his "secret weapon." "He is the most underestimated guy here. He is a genius, self-taught electrical, mechanical, hydraulic expert," said Prince.

Dehart's contributions to developing and testing new targeting systems would be critical to the organization. Targeting systems, not training, would pull the company out of the red. Blackwater couldn't make a big profit if every transaction required staff time and the use of its facilities. Why not try manufacturing? Training alone was hardly generating enough to make back the initial investment and the costs it had taken to run the company for nearly three years. Prince started to look closer at contracting with the government as a way to generate even more revenue.

As the pressure mounted for the business to be profitable, friction among the management team began to show. "In the beginning the company was very different; it was just a bunch of good old boys out to do some really good training and change the industry standard," remembered one former manager. "It really was like 'Erik's playground' in a lot of ways. He had the money. The change happened when he started putting pressure on to meet financial goals. Erik needed the company to be profitable and wanted to turn a profit fast."

The men started to disagree about strategy. Al Clark was eventually let go. Dale McClellan decided to leave as well. Ken Viera also struggled with the direction in which he felt Prince wanted to move the company, and he argued about some of Prince's hiring decisions. Finally, Viera left Blackwater in June 1999.

THAT SAME MONTH, Erik Prince became a father for the fourth time when Joan gave birth to Erik Xavier, whom they called X. He joined the growing family that included older brother Christian and older sisters Sophia and Isabella. A year after X's birth, Erik and Joan moved their growing family to Virginia, but something had been nagging at Prince's young wife. "She kept complaining that her lower back hurt," recalled Prince. "We had been moving boxes and stuff, and I figured she must have pulled a muscle, because that's how she described it. I don't know if she just didn't want to acknowledge that the pain wasn't normal, but it got worse and worse and just wouldn't go away." But with a new baby and a growing, changing company on their hands, Joan didn't pay much attention to the pain.

Prince also relocated his holding company, The Prince Group, to a Virginia high-rise. The holding company allowed him to better manage a parts manufacturing facility he inherited from his father as well as his new ventures, like Blackwater. The central location would allow him to be closer to Moyock, North Carolina, and the Blackwater training facility. The Prince Group was also just a stone's throw from Washington's halls of power and the Central Intelligence Agency in Langley, Virginia. Business was already picking up. Blackwater had been entered into the General Services contracting database for government-approved goods and services. It was a huge step for the company, as it meant Blackwater was now a trusted government contractor in the running for more lucrative, long-term federal contracts.

As business was picking up for Blackwater at home, trouble was brewing more than seven thousand miles away, in a country about twice the size of Wyoming. Yemen sits strategically on the Gulf of Aden in the Middle East. What income the country is able to generate is based largely on dwindling oil reserves. With no official Coast Guard to speak of, the gulf waters are notorious for piracy and smuggling. The State Department warned that Yemen, in particular, was also becoming a haven for terrorists. Still, the U.S. Navy had used the port as a refueling point dozens of times.

In August 2000, a 505-foot Arleigh Burke–class destroyer, the USS *Cole,* was deployed to the Mediterranean and Red Sea. It had scarcely been in the area two months when it entered Aden Harbor to refuel. As the *Cole* glided into port, a small boat sped toward it. Onboard were two suicide bombers and enough explosives to blow a forty-by-sixty-foot hole in the side of the mighty destroyer. Initial reports estimated that the amount of explosives packed in that boat was equivalent to a truck bomb. Seventeen sailors were killed; thirty-nine more were wounded. Reaction from the White House was swift.

"We will do whatever it takes, for as long as it takes, to find those who killed our sailors and hold them accountable," said President Bill Clinton. Teams were sent from the Department of Defense, FBI, and State Department to Yemen to investigate. The president also called for U.S. ships to pull out of the port and ordered U.S. land forces to increase their security.

Erik Prince was listening. He knew the attack had likely exposed the weaknesses in the Navy's force protection structure. The Navy now faced a very real terror threat to its fleet around the world. Many of the sailors onboard the USS *Cole* had scarcely even fired a weapon—not that there would have been time to stop the attack—but it did highlight a stunning lack of preparedness.

As intelligence officials began looking closer at the attack and putting the pieces together, a familiar name popped up: Osama bin Laden. U.S. investigators were looking at similarities between the USS *Cole* attack and the bombing of the two U.S.

embassies in East Africa just two years before. The attacks had
been planned well ahead of time. There were indications of safe
houses being used and personnel moving in and out of the area.
America's new enemy was highly sophisticated and stealthy, and
the number of its potential targets was enormous.

Within months, the Navy came knocking on Prince's door.
The seamen had a new, very detailed training program, but they
needed Prince to provide the facilities and the trainers for it.
Prince understood the magnitude of the task and the enormous
need for training that would prepare sailors for the very real
threat awaiting them. "The sailors who were guarding that ship
were, I won't give you the level of detail how bad it was, but it
was bad," he said.

The Navy was Blackwater's first truly big customer, and the
contract with the Navy was the beginning of a boom in demand.
In addition to the Blackwater campus in Moyock, Prince soon
leased a facility in California, to try to keep up with the demands
of the contract. "That kind of volume running through a facility
here and through a facility out in California greatly cranked up
our demand, so we were running hard in that direction," recalled
Prince.

Prince, like many others, believed strongly that the military
had been preparing for the wrong war. The Pentagon had under-
gone significant cutbacks in troop levels in the 1990s. "The military trained for sixty years to fight a Soviet rifle regiment force,"
said Prince. "To shift the military to fight the insurgency in a very
different land meant there were a lot of folks that needed training; they needed small-unit focus on tactics and capabilities."

Prince was proud of his ability to "lean over his skis," antici-
pate where the next need would come from, then figure out how
Blackwater could accommodate. He still wasn't close to recoup-

ing the almost $6 million he had poured into the company, but he could see black ink in Blackwater's near future.

THERE WAS MUCH TO CELEBRATE at Blackwater at the beginning of 2001. For Prince personally, however, 2001 began with a blow. Finally following up on the pain that had been intensifying the summer before, Joan had an X-ray that showed something unusual. A few days later, an MRI and bone scan confirmed the worst. Her cancer was back.

"We'd been through a bunch of that stuff before," recalled Prince, "and usually the operators are pretty chipper and happy to talk to you, and you kind of get the wink and the nod that everything's OK. They didn't this time. Her doc said the cancer had metastasized and was all through her pelvis and spine." It was devastating news for a woman just in her early thirties, with four young children. Her prognosis was grim and would require treatments that would see her mobility and energy levels slowly deteriorate. By September the chemotherapy was taking its toll.

ON SEPTEMBER 11, 2001, Cofer Black sat in his office at CIA headquarters in Langley, Virginia. CIA director George Tenet had named Black director of the agency's Counterterrorist Center just two years earlier. A classically trained spy, Black had spent much of his career in Africa, partly as the CIA's station chief in Khartoum, Sudan, from 1993 to 1995. Osama bin Laden was already a person of interest at the CIA even then, when he was thought to be a key funding conduit for terrorist organizations. Indeed, bin Laden had tried to kill him in an elaborate attack that had been foiled.

There were several people in Black's office that morning when a colleague poked his head in to say that a plane had just flown into the north tower of the World Trade Center. Within minutes, Black was on the phone with a colleague in New York, who was briefing him on the incident. That's when a second plane hit the south tower. Black knew the day the agency had been dreading had just arrived.

"In my personal and professional opinion, it took me about 0.56 seconds to figure out that this was part of the attack plan we had been expecting," said Black.

Within just two days of the attacks, the agency had put together a team to root out bin Laden in Afghanistan, and it would mean rooting out the Taliban government as well. CIA teams met up with the Northern Alliance to tell them to prepare for war. Black told one of the team leaders to bring back bin Laden's head in a box of dry ice. While many may have thought it was a joke, Black was sincere. There were times in the past when the agency had thought it had bin Laden, only to be disappointed. This time, Black wanted tangible proof that the Saudi was dead. Instead of taking a syringe and comparing DNA analysis, he wanted something more visually compelling.

Erik Prince was on his way to get a haircut when he heard on the radio that a plane had flown into one of the World Trade Center towers. As he walked into the barber shop, he told the barbers there to turn on the television. He was sitting in the barber chair when the second plane struck.

Prince's life shifted into overdrive. He and Joan flew to New York just days after the attack so that she could undergo chemotherapy. He took a walk down to the World Trade Center site and flashed his military ID to get a closer look at the devastation: "That made it sink in all that much more. It just changed reality."

Prince started making calls to people he knew in government agencies, including a call to the then–executive director of the CIA, A. B. "Buzzy" Krongard. It was a move that paid off. The United States was about to invade Afghanistan, and the CIA, not the Pentagon, would lead the effort. Cofer Black called Henry Crumpton back from Australia to accept the assignment to lead the CIA's operation on the ground. As the agency's chief of mission in Afghanistan, Crumpton knew the country well. Two years earlier, the CIA had sent covert teams into Afghanistan because there was concern that al-Qaeda was planning a large-scale attack against the United States.

The plan this time was to go into the country with the Northern Alliance and other Afghan allies and make a push to Kabul. The operation was a little too successful, though, and the teams got to the Afghan capital months faster than Crumpton had anticipated. He could see that the Taliban were far weaker than the agency had expected. With U.S. operatives now in Kabul and the Taliban no longer a significant threat, the focus turned once again to hunting down al-Qaeda. That would mean a lot of movement in a country that still presented a significant danger of reprisal attacks. The agency would need protection, but it simply didn't have the bodies to provide it. It had tried hiring locals to do the job and had been woefully unsatisfied with the results. Krongard had made a trip to Afghanistan himself and was concerned either that the locals weren't up to the task or, his greater fear, that they might collaborate with the Taliban, and the base could be overrun. The U.S. military didn't have the bodies for static security either, so the agency hired out. Krongard pushed for Blackwater to fill the role.

Blackwater had already been hosting CIA personnel at its Moyock facility. The agency had a steady stream of special activities people, protection details, and case officers getting training at Blackwater in everything from driving skills to shooting skills. When Krongard visited the facility to get a better idea of the training his people were receiving, he spent some time shooting with his guys and sat down for a conversation with Gary Jackson. Jackson suggested that Krongard meet with Prince, who lived in the D.C. area. Prince and Krongard immediately struck up a relationship. Krongard's own son was a Navy SEAL, and the executive director found himself impressed with Prince's membership in the elite club.

"I was really impressed that someone of his means had gone through the program," recalled Krongard. "He didn't have to do it."

Once 9/11 occurred, Prince had no trouble getting the CIA's executive director on the line.

Within days, Blackwater received an urgent and compelling contract from the agency to provide security for the CIA station in Kabul and various installations where the CIA was holding detainees. The contract would be renewed several times and would provide a consistent and profitable stream of revenue for years to come.

It was a boost for the business, even if it was a mad scramble to find the bodies to fulfill the contract.

"It was a blast," said Jackson. "We just called eighteen buddies up. I'll never forget the big Marine out at Pendleton. I called him up, and he's in a driving course. I said, 'Hey, I've got a job.' 'Cool.' Errrrrk, I hear tires screeching. He says, 'Oh, I'm teaching a driving course.'"

It wasn't tough for Jackson to pull together the initial team of men, and Prince went to oversee the project personally. It was his first trip to Afghanistan. As a former SEAL, he had spent time in rough locations before, but Kabul was unlike anything he'd seen.

"Everything was kind of in flux in the capital," recalled Prince. "We were just trying to figure out who was doing what where and what the military was doing. It was a challenge."

Prince himself joined in one rotation of guards and even helped construct a detention facility. It included mundane activities like stringing barbed wire and wiring lights.

"The contract [with the CIA] called for providing static guard services and that's all," said Prince. "In reality what they got was a whole lot more than that from construction and us helping them build out part of one facility. We saved them millions and millions of dollars because our guys truly multitasked."

Business was finally picking up. In October 2001 Prince decided to put Gary Jackson in charge of Blackwater. Jackson had been a loyal supporter and had shown Prince his dedication to growing the company by never saying no. It was a personal motto. Jackson showed none of the resistance that others had over the company's mission, and whether it should stick to its roots as a training facility or branch out wherever opportunity took them, namely, the security business.

"The joke is I got the position through attrition; there was nobody left," said Jackson. The reality is that he was always the company's biggest booster, after Prince.

Jackson, like Prince, had been a Navy SEAL. It was an important test of patriotism and endurance. Jackson had even written his own book about what it meant: ninety-five stories from his time in the service, under the title *There We Were*. It was never picked up by a major publisher, but Jackson sold some copies on the Internet. Most of the stories told of escapades with women or of SEALs proving themselves by, for example, beating up drunk Marines.

By the time Prince made the decision to promote Jackson to the number one spot, Jackson was ready. He felt as if he had been preparing for the job for nearly four years. He had fulfilled just about every other role at the fledgling company and thought the move to be a natural progression. But even his enthusiasm would be tested by the explosive growth the company was about to experience. Prince and Jackson would need a lot more help.

Chris Taylor was a former Recon Marine, the Marines' version of Special Forces. After leaving active duty, he was having trouble finding work. The attacks of September 11 had taken a toll on the economy. His best friend, an instructor at Blackwater, got him in the door. Taylor's first assignment was as an instructor in the Navy's border protection fundamentals training program. He was working at the company's ship trainer facility one day when Erik Prince rode up on a mountain bike. "He said, 'You're a Force Recon Marine with an MBA?'" recounted Taylor. "I said, 'Yeah,' and he goes, 'You're running the ship trainer?' and I said, 'Yeah,' and he said, 'Why don't you come and talk to me when the day's over? Maybe there's something else we can have you do.'"

Taylor interviewed that afternoon with both Jackson and Prince, and the two men hired him as the director of Blackwater Target Systems, working alongside Jim Dehart. While Dehart had a history of building and designing shoot houses and ranges, he didn't have a business background. That's where Taylor came in. The company was soon awarded a contract from the Marine Corps for marksmanship competitive training ranges at Parris Island.

While Prince himself won't talk about how much money the

company was making at any given time, various reports by congressional committees set the company's revenue around $3.4 million in 2002. Prince would only say the figure is "a little high."

BY 2003 JACKSON and Prince knew they needed a more structured business model to accommodate the expanding demand for their services. They created vice presidents to oversee particular divisions. Taylor became vice president for strategic initiatives.

The changes came quickly, which meant a lot of on-the-job training.

"We lived Blackwater twenty-four hours a day," said Taylor. "We did amazing things, and we were getting attention, but most importantly, we were actually having an impact."

Word was spreading rapidly through government ranks about this new company. Ricky Chambers heard about it while working for the FBI in Africa.

"At the time the FBI, the State Department, and other agencies were looking into a report that a 737 was missing in East Africa, and there were reports of another terrorist attack using a plane to run into a Western target," he recalled. "One of the possible solutions at the time was to consider using a military or private company with individuals who could operate a weapon system to shoot the plane out of the sky. Blackwater was on a list that I was given the responsibility to short-list and make inquiries of their capabilities."

Ultimately, Chambers said, Blackwater didn't get the contract, and the threat subsided, but personal pressures had led him to look for other work. He started asking around at Blackwater. In 2003 he became the first federal law enforcement agent to leave the bureau and go to work for Blackwater.

CHAPTER 4

How to Rent a War

HIRING SOLDIERS to fight other people's wars is an ancient practice, from antiquity to Renaissance Italy to, indeed, the American Revolution. The British hired German soldiers from the Hesse region to take up guns on their behalf during the Revolutionary War. Friedrich von Steuben, born in the Magdeburg region of what is now Germany, fought for the freedom of the colonies. Once the war was won, his service was honored with U.S. citizenship and a statue that today sits in Lafayette Park across the street from the White House in Washington, D.C.

But in more recent times, corporations who hire out professionals to support military missions are often accused of "war profiteering." The fees charged by companies have come under scrutiny and raised questions about whether the practice has gone too far, and whether the U.S. government still has a handle on what "inherently governmental" truly means.

Today's hired help has responded to criticism in much the same way, reminding critics that they are performing work at the

request of the U.S. government. Most of the larger companies
are well aware of the public perception, and many of them don't
like the term *mercenary*. Thus, the term *private military contractor*
has taken hold. Love them or hate them, the truth is, no modern
democratic government attempts to handle all supply, logistics,
and manufacturing needs strictly through the public sector. The
United States is no exception.

In the early 1990s, Dick Cheney, then secretary of defense,
issued a multimillion-dollar contract to the Texas-based company Brown & Root to study the benefits of using private contractors to do jobs once handled by the military: everything from
building bases to feeding troops. Several months later, Brown &
Root was awarded the Army's first Logistics Civil Augmentation
Program contract, which would eventually become the model
for the industry. LOGCAP, as it was known, set a new trend in
how the U.S. military would support itself on the battlefield. In
theory, troops would be freed from the mundane so they could
concentrate on more serious efforts. Cheney's embrace of the
report signaled an important shift in how the U.S. war machine
functioned. There was concern, though, among critics that relationships between private companies and the government were
too close, a concern not helped by the fact that after leaving
the government, Cheney became the CEO of Halliburton, the
parent company of Brown & Root. According to the Center for
Public Integrity, Cheney oversaw the near doubling of the company's contracts with the U.S. government, reaching awards as
high as $2.3 billion.

U.S. contracting was initially meant to be logistical in nature.
In Vietnam, the U.S. military relied on private companies to build
bases and handle other noncombat tasks. The Pentagon had more
recently employed private contractors in Colombia to help boost

its total force working in support of drug eradication. There was supposed to be a line between the military and its contractors when it came to combat versus support. Of course, there were always hazards, and the line could blur. While contractors were generally paid handsomely, there was always a risk.

An unforgettable example of contractors at risk happened in Colombia in 2003. Marc Gonsalves, a former intelligence officer in the Air Force, had switched to a far better paying private sector job, working for a company called California Microwave Systems, a then subsidiary of the U.S. defense contractor Northrop Grumman. One February morning in 2003, Gonsalves and three of his contractor colleagues, Thomas Howes, Keith Stansell, and Tom Janis, climbed into a Cessna 206 for a flight over remote areas of the Colombian jungle, many of which were controlled by FARC (the Revolutionary Armed Forces of Colombia) rebels. The U.S. government believed that FARC was sustaining itself by trading in narcotics.

Not long into the flight, the plane developed engine trouble. Within minutes, the single-engine Cessna slammed into a remote Colombian hillside. The men survived the crash, but the plane had gone down near a FARC unit, and armed members of the group quickly surrounded the crash site. Copilot Tom Janis and a Colombian army sergeant were shot and killed on the spot. Gonsalves, Stansell, and Howes were taken hostage and marched at gunpoint into the jungle.

Hours turned to days, days to weeks. There was no plan to get the Americans back. The State Department kept in close contact with the families of the men at first, but eventually there was nothing to report, nothing to say. The United States considered FARC a terrorist organization, so there would be no direct negotiations for the hostages' release.

That meant a long confinement for Gonsalves, Stansell, and Howes in the rugged mountain region of Colombia. The rebels demanded that the Colombian government release several of its own prisoners in exchange for their freedom; the government refused.

The government began laying the groundwork for a rescue. It wasn't only the Americans they were trying to free—it was also fourteen other hostages, including former Colombian presidential candidate Ingrid Betancourt.

It would take five years, but the rescue was thrilling. Colombian intelligence agencies had managed to infiltrate the highest levels of the FARC leadership and launched a dramatic rescue attempt that included convincing lower-level FARC guards to turn the hostages over to a rescue organization that was really a group of undercover special agents. What followed was enormous relief and jubilation, yet amid the celebration, it was easy to overlook what the hostages had gone through. The U.S. government cared about the American hostages working on their behalf, but not enough to stage its own rescue attempt. It would have been risky; the FARC had promised to kill the hostages if it had even a hint of a rescue attempt. There was a valuable lesson in Stansell, Gonsalves, and Howe's story: although contractors often benefit financially from selling their skills to the private marketplace, they also suffer the risks of putting themselves in harm's way at the behest of a mere corporation.

COLOMBIA WAS RIFE with hostage taking and ransom operations, but Iraq soon seized the international spotlight as a killing ground for hostages, especially contractors. The U.S.-led invasion, beginning in March 2003, led to a swift overthrow of

Saddam Hussein's regime. Yet there were top-level concerns inside the Pentagon that the United States didn't have enough boots on the ground to maintain a lasting peace. The Pentagon had spent more than a decade downsizing its force; the reality was that the war machine just wasn't as big as it had once been.

Retired lieutenant general Jay Garner was assigned the unenviable task of overseeing reconstruction as the senior civil administrator in Iraq. There were some in the State Department who didn't think that a military man should be in that role. Garner, who would later talk about missteps made early on that included not having enough troops in Baghdad and not putting more of an effort into communications with the Iraqi people (Iraqis continued to get most of their news about the occupation from Al Jazeera), was replaced after just one month.

The White House called on retired ambassador L. Paul Bremer to take control of the newly formed Coalition Provisional Authority (CPA). His task was to facilitate the eventual handing over of control to an Iraqi government, but there was much to be done before that could happen.

Bremer came out of retirement to take on the task and handpicked the men he wanted at his side: retired ambassador Clay McManaway and Ambassador Patrick Kennedy, whom he had worked with previously at the State Department.

Kennedy was a career diplomat, with a quiet but firm way of getting things done. He was working at the time at the United Nations for Ambassador John Negroponte and went "on loan" to the Department of Defense so that he could assist Bremer in Baghdad. But it was clear even before he arrived that while Bremer, as head of the CPA, would have sweeping authority in the country, he would not have authority over the 170,000 coalition troops. That was a job that fell to General Ricardo Sanchez.

Sanchez watched as the State Department brought on contractors to help with security, and he grew uneasy at the potential conflict with his own troops.

The State Department's Diplomatic Security Service was never meant to be a war zone security force, and it lacked the personnel the department needed in Iraq to keep diplomats and visitors safe. Yet for Bremer to do his job, it was imperative that he have a team of professionals trained in personal security detail. Initially, the job fell to the Army's Criminal Investigation Command, one of the few divisions of the Pentagon that had personnel trained in this kind of close protection. On that team were two Blackwater contractors, both of them ex–Navy SEALs. The men had been requested by higher-ups in the Pentagon for the Bremer detail based on their work in Afghanistan. Thanks to its target systems, Blackwater was already on the government's General Services Administration (GSA) schedule—which meant it was an approved government contractor. Prince got the contract under an urgent and compelling need provision, which meant Blackwater didn't have to compete for the deal.

Erik Prince first met Paul Bremer at the Pentagon as the new CPA leader was preparing to leave for Iraq. Bremer needed to be fitted for body armor, and Prince needed to be sure his highest-profile client was going to be happy. Prince also knew the contract was an important opportunity for Blackwater to cement its image inside the Pentagon. The CPA would be in charge of congressional delegations and visiting dignitaries in a place where suicide bombings and mortar attacks were not unusual, and the body count was ticking up day by day. The coalition operated inside a fortified Green Zone, but rebuilding the country couldn't be done from inside the zone alone.

With insurgents ramping up attacks in and around Baghdad,

Kennedy realized early on that his team needed more security personnel than the Army was able to deliver. "I reported to Washington that the threat level is going up and that we needed additional CID personnel," said Kennedy.

Kennedy had spoken to General Peter Pace, vice chairman of the Joint Chiefs of Staff, in early to mid-2003, but "the answer came back that we simply do not have any more personnel. The U.S. Army's major responsibility is to project force, to attack. They don't train lots of people in personal protection, and so there is only a small cadre of Army, Air Force, and Navy investigative service personnel who are trained in protection."

The Pentagon's only option was contracting out the work. "The Pentagon told me, we simply cannot get you any more personnel, and we're going to send you contractors," recalled Kennedy. "I said, 'OK, are you sure? I can't execute a contract out here.' They said, 'No, no, no, we'll do all the contract work, and we'll send you the contractors.'"

While technically on a Department of Defense contract, the contractors were nevertheless assigned to Paul Bremer, and they were civilians. It was an arrangement that made General Sanchez uncomfortable, not only because of the nature of the work being performed by the contractors, but also because the military often wasn't told about contractor movements in Iraq. The military was having a hard time keeping track of who was where. There were a growing number of private contractors supporting the military's logistical needs, with no clear way for those people to efficiently communicate with the military command.

"The challenge became the tremendously large requirement and the quality control and then the actual oversight of all of that that started to flow into the country at such a rapid expansion," said Sanchez.

While Blackwater wasn't the only government contractor getting work in Iraq, there was one thing that set it apart from the
competition. Because of Prince's private wealth, the company was
able to provide the equipment, not just the personnel, to support
the contract. Sanchez was witnessing the buildup of what looked
an awful lot like a shadow army. Blackwater already had more than
a half dozen helicopters and was on its way to acquiring more.

"There were significant challenges because they were very
much an independent operating entity; they had assets from
Hawk helicopters down to the individual little teams. I think probably the biggest challenge we were having was just being able to
coordinate and synchronize with them, because they didn't have
the mechanisms in the country to maintain the right situational
awareness, the right linkages to our forces on the ground. It was
always a constant battle making sure we had that visibility on
their activities," said Sanchez.

The struggle over just who had control of the contractors and
their weapons led to contentious conversations between Sanchez
and Kennedy. Sanchez believed it was critical for CENTCOM
(Central Command) to play a larger role in the coordination
of communication between troops and private armed convoys
moving around the country. Kennedy disagreed.

"Mr. Kennedy really believed that they had the authority to
command those assets, which was a significant challenge for me,
because they didn't have the skills and the staff capacity to be
able to do actual operations and then synchronize war fighting
forces, which is what they were," said Sanchez.

"Rick and I had several conversations," said Kennedy, "and my
view was always, 'We do have a clear line of demarcation here;
Rick Sanchez commands the troops, and Jerry [Paul] Bremer
commands the civilians, and that is the clear demarcation line.'"

The coordination of contractors would prove to be a never-ending challenge for Sanchez, one that would lead to ugly confrontations between troops and contractors, many of whom were retired military making more than twice as much as their military counterparts. The Department of Defense and the Department of State fought many bureaucratic skirmishes in Iraq. In this case, critics would say the State Department wielded its own private army.

"This is a question that continues to hound me to this day," said Sanchez. "There was a mind-set that was almost unexplainable about maintaining this separation with the military assets on the ground that permeated just about everything that was going on in the country, from the building of security forces to the actual combat operations and initiatives."

IF THERE WAS CONFUSION and poor communication over contractors on the ground in Iraq, there was even more back at the Pentagon. Little had been done to prepare for the onslaught of contracts that were coming. The contracting offices were woefully short of experienced personnel, and in the beginning, there was no clear structure in place for dealing with them.

A former Department of Defense (DoD) official who was heavily involved in the acquisition process at the Pentagon but didn't want to be identified said the requests for contractors were piling up in a hurry. "You had the Pentagon requiring all these things for Iraq, but there's no contractual infrastructure."

According to the former official, "When you get into other things like security, there was no infrastructure contractually, so you had all these organizations saying we need this convoy support to protect these bases. They would come up with all these requirements and say, 'Oh, by the way, we need it really, really, tomorrow,' or 'We really need it in a week from now,' but they're multimillion-dollar contracts."

The urgency combined with a lack of experience with contractors had the military in a bind. Contracting officers were rotated as often as every six months, giving them precious little time to develop a comprehensive understanding of the process and requirements.

According to the former DoD official, contracting officers who at one time handled contracts for things like facility maintenance that might include cutting grass were now wrapping their arms around multimillion-dollar security contracts that dealt with armed private civilians. "The exposure by the contracting officers to that kind of contracting was extremely limited to begin with," said the source.

THE PENTAGON'S CONFUSION, the State Department's hunger, and the blurring boundaries of activity added up to a jackpot for Erik Prince. His security division was booming in Afghanistan and had become its own protective army for the State Department in Iraq. Blackwater Target Systems was making a growing profit. The new aviation business was poised for takeoff.

Yet Prince's life at home stood in sharp contrast to his success at work.

Joan had been fighting her cancer since its ferocious return in 2001, and it wasn't going well. The disease had spread and was putting up more of a fight than she could handle.

Prince recalled watching his wife's health deteriorate as she tried to fight the disease that was slowly killing her. On Mother's Day, he helped Joan shave off her blond hair. He was a dedicated husband watching as his wife and the mother of his four children slipped closer to death.

On the other hand, he had a terrible secret that would only add to his family's pain.

A young woman named Joanna Houck had worked for Erik and Joan as a nanny when they were living in Michigan. When the couple and their children moved to Virginia, Houck moved to take a job at Blackwater's Moyock campus, where Prince worked several days a week. It became obvious to some working there that the relationship between Houck and Prince had become personal. In fact, they were secretly involved in a relationship. At some point, Joan found out and, according to one person close to her, insisted that "that woman" be kept away from her children.

After years of trying to fight it, Joan Nicole Prince lost her battle to cancer in June 2003. She was surrounded by her family and friends when she died. Her children were just eight, seven, five, and three years old.

Some of Prince's colleagues were shocked when Houck showed up at Joan's funeral. They saw the affair as deeply hypocritical, but it was worse to flaunt it. Yet perhaps it was too late to try to hide the relationship: Houck was already several months pregnant with Prince's child.

Prince would later only admit that he didn't handle Joan's struggle with cancer very well.

The affair was a disturbing revelation for some close to Prince. They knew him as a deeply religious man dedicated to his family, and the affair was inconsistent with the man they thought they knew. It also caused deep divides in the relationship between Prince and members of Joan's family. Prince was extremely uncomfortable discussing the subject, saying only, "If you do the math on their birth dates, some of them don't add up perfectly, but they're all great little kids."

Prince's fifth child was born a few months later, and he eventually did what he called "the right thing" and married Joanna Houck, but "merging" his two families would prove to be challenging at best.

THERE WAS ANOTHER RELATIONSHIP in Prince's life that developed as he dealt with the death of his wife. Gary Jackson had become his main confidant, ally, friend, and counsel. The relationship was both praised and criticized by people inside the company, with some saying that Jackson held too much sway over Prince. Those who praised them said the two knew what they wanted and how to get it. Either way, it was a relationship both men deemed unique.

"Sometimes we look at each other, and we try to figure it out," explained Jackson. "I'm older, only a dozen years older than he is, but I'm still a dozen years older than he is."

Jackson came into Prince's life after the death of Edgar Prince. The relationship had been described as part brotherly, part fatherly. Both men were Navy SEALs, and Jackson saw a natural fit. "He is a visionary," said Jackson. "My strength is that I'm a natural-born entrepreneur. I try to provide solutions that will produce revenue; that's my gig." And that's just what Prince wanted for Blackwater. Jackson had become a close personal friend who still addressed the boss as "sir."

"I'm not the guy that just says, 'Yes, yes, yes, yes, sir.' I'm the guy who comes back and says, 'No frickin way, sir; we cannot do that.'"

The company operated on a unique chain of command. Without a board of directors to answer to, the buck always stopped with Prince, whose only limitation was financial—and that hadn't proven much of a limitation at all.

One thing Prince and Jackson agreed on in 2003 was the need for the company to grow if it wanted to take advantage of the opportunities in an explosively expanding marketplace. There were dozens and dozens of new private firms popping up and bidding for DoD contracts. Blackwater, like other companies, went looking for men with valuable inside experience.

Mike Rush was on the bureaucratic treadmill at Homeland Security when Blackwater came knocking. He had spent twenty-three years in the Navy before he accepted a job as the deputy director for security operations at Blackwater, putting him in charge of getting contractors outfitted, trained, and ready to deploy. It was a big job. In addition to the Pentagon detail, the company had work for the CIA that had expanded from Afghanistan to include Iraq as well. Blackwater had some thirty men assigned to protect members of the Iraq Survey Group (ISG), headed by former weapons inspector David Kay and charged with finding weapons of mass destruction in Iraq after the invasion.

The ISG was divided up and assigned to sectors where members searched for evidence of chemical and biological weapons. Many in Washington expected that the country would be littered with stockpiles of WMD, but the ISG teams found next to nothing, despite nearly six months of effort. By this point, in Iraq, Blackwater was working for the State Department, DoD, and the CIA, and Rush was in charge of the training for all of Blackwater's contracts.

At first, Rush found the quick decision-making at Blackwater to be a refreshing change from the bureaucracy at Homeland Security. "It was a gung-ho little team with a fight attitude, and scrappy, because they really didn't have a lot," Rush said.

He, like every other executive at the company, was expected to help attract new business in addition to performing his duties overseeing the training of new recruits. But despite his first impressions, Rush would later come to believe that the relationship between Prince and Jackson wasn't always best for the business. He came to see that their "can-do" attitude sometimes meant that they would make up their minds quickly, he says, accepting some people seemingly without question, while rejecting others without any obvious reason. "Once they made up their mind about somebody, there was no middle ground," said Rush. For Prince, that was part of the appeal of having a short chain of command.

Blackwater had become an interesting hybrid of corporate and military. For some employees, Blackwater was nothing less than a patriotic mission, on a par with the Army itself. For others, it was a business, just another way to make a profit. As the company grew, some felt the buck seekers came to outnumber the missionaries. For Prince, of course, Blackwater was both a mission and a means of enrichment. There had been times when he had to dip into his personal fortune just to keep it running. "Whether you know it or not, there were a lot of lean years there. In fact, one of the worst times was when we hadn't been paid by the government for many months," said Rush. "We actually had to go through Erik's financial guy and get his assets out of some of Erik's portfolio so we could make payroll. Then, literally hours after we did that, the government came through with two or three months of invoices in arrears that hadn't been paid up."

Despite the financial ups and downs, Prince was focusing on expanding the company's security services. He also knew that with the kinds of high-ticket contracts he was interested in, he needed to bring Blackwater out of the mom-and-pop organization it had started out as, and shape and form it into something that looked more like a Fortune 500 company. But he didn't want to organize it like a typical Fortune 500 firm. He continued to be its sole owner, and he had no interest in involving a board of directors. Prince made up his own mind about whom to trust, and about whom to hire for top-level positions. His old buddy and fellow SEAL Bill Mathews fit the bill. "I remember when he called me," said Mathews. "He was looking for people that he knew and trusted and had some sort of advanced degree and business experience. I'm a lawyer and was general counsel for a company in the Midwest."

Mathews was hired mainly to establish critical business infrastructure in the booming business. With more employees, Blackwater needed a human resources department, an accounting department, and a risk management team.

"When I came in, it was a very young company being run primarily by the big guys from the Special Operations community," said Mathews. "I was kind of a way to help those guys segue to develop more of a business infrastructure, the boring stuff."

The "boring stuff" like risk management would prove anything but.

THE AUGUST HEAT in Baghdad is intense, with temperatures often reaching into the triple digits. On August 19, 2003, the United Nations' chief envoy to Iraq, Sérgio Vieira de Mello, was working in an office set up in the Canal Hotel, which doubled as the international organization's Baghdad headquarters. Security in the Baghdad area was high. Just two weeks earlier, a car bomb detonated outside the Jordanian embassy, killing ten people. Intelligence officials were coming to understand the extent to which Iraq's borders, left largely unmanned during the aftermath of the invasion, had been infiltrated by al-Qaeda terrorists, who were now launching attacks against a wide range of targets. Just how dangerous the country had become became obvious in the moments after a truck pulled up to the Canal Hotel, just under the window of the office where Vieira de Mello was working.

Pat Kennedy was across town in a meeting with a visiting Senate delegation led by Senator John McCain. Paul Bremer was addressing the group when someone slipped into the room and handed Kennedy a note saying only that there had been a bombing at the United Nations compound. Kennedy showed the note to Bremer, then wrote, "Get me more information," and gave it to the aide. A few moments passed before the aide returned, saying that he had been unable to reach anyone by phone. Kennedy checked his cell phone and wrote down a couple of phone numbers of UN contacts and sent the aide to try again. When the aide came back empty-handed, Kennedy excused himself from the meeting.

"I whispered to Jerry [Paul Bremer], 'I think I'm leaving,'" recalled Kennedy. He got up, left the room, grabbed his radio equipment and flak jacket, and headed for the UN compound. What he found was utter devastation. As Kennedy's vehicle approached the Canal Hotel, he could see smoke rising above the surrounding buildings. As he got even closer, he could see that an entire chunk of the building was gone. Adjacent to the hotel was the headquarters of the Third Armored Cavalry Regiment, whose personnel had already secured a perimeter around the area and were searching through the chunks of concrete. U.S. Army medevac helicopters had arrived to transport the wounded to the Army hospital.

As Kennedy surveyed the damage, it brought to mind images of another bombing, that of the American embassy in Nairobi. He reached for his phone to brief Bremer.

"I forwarded the news that there was serious damage, a number of dead, many injured, that Sérgio [Vieira] de Mello was trapped in the rubble. I called him several more times to keep him abreast of it," said Kennedy. "He and several members of the governing council came to the site about an hour or so later, while rescue operations were ongoing."

The rubble was so deep that it took hours to reach those buried underneath. Searchers eventually recovered the bodies of Vieira de Mello and twenty-one others. Investigators later determined that the truck parked outside the hotel was laden with more than 1,500 pounds of explosives.

By the end of the month, the Pentagon's task to provide security for Bremer and his staff was officially settled. Blackwater had been awarded a $27 million contract, this time directly from the State Department.

Sometime after the contract was awarded, Prince himself made a trip to Baghdad, as he often did, to visit the client and make sure all was going smoothly. His company had grown so quickly that many of the people who worked for him had never even met the boyish-looking former SEAL. When Prince arrived at the Blackwater house where the contractors were staying, the men were moving furniture, and one of them, not recognizing Prince, ordered him to grab a sofa and lend a hand. On the way up the stairs, he commented on Prince's physique: "Hey, that's a pretty nice ass; what do you feed it?" It wasn't until the men set the sofa down that Prince introduced himself as the owner of the fast-growing company.

BY THE END OF 2003, Blackwater had built a database of hundreds of men, many of whom were deployed in Iraq. It also had dozens of men on contract to the CIA and a fleet of aircraft deployed for the Department of Defense. Blackwater was becoming a sprawling giant that would grow to around two thousand employees, not counting the men who were deployed on contracts. Estimated revenues were soaring to the hundreds of millions.

The government's ability to manage the explosive growth of private contractors it had employed wasn't keeping up. The big companies like Halliburton would often subcontract services to smaller companies, who often in turn subcontracted again. That's how Blackwater ended up working for Regency Hotel and the Hospital of Kuwait in March 2004. Regency was subcontracted by a company called ESS Support Services Worldwide to provide food and catering supplies to U.S. troops. ESS, in turn, was a subcontractor to KBR, a subsidiary of Halliburton, which held the actual contract with the Pentagon.

The Blackwater part of the contract called for security services for the "movement of ESS's staff." It was a job that would prove significantly dangerous, given the uptick in insurgent attacks on reconstruction convoys in the country.

CHAPTER 5

The Bridge in Iraq

HAREEQ, GHAREEQ WA SHARHATTA ALA AL-TAREEQ is a saying common in Arab cultures, meaning that among the worst ways to die is by fire, water, or being dragged through the streets.

THE IRAQI CITY OF FALLUJAH is some thirty miles to the west of the capital, Baghdad. As part of the "Sunni Triangle" that spanned west of Baghdad and to the north, it had become a place of more frequent attacks against U.S. troops by March 2004. U.S. Marines stationed at nearby Camp Fallujah wouldn't go near the downtown district, unless they were heavily armed and traveling in numbers. With no real U.S. presence to speak of, the town itself had become a haven for insurgents to gather and plan their attacks.

Fallujah certainly wasn't where Scott Helvenston thought he would find himself as he packed up his bags in Southern California and hurried to catch a plane on his way to the Blackwater training facility in Moyock, North Carolina. Helvenston had been a Navy SEAL attached to SEAL Team 5 in Coronado, California, and later to SEAL Team 4 at the naval base near Virginia Beach, Virginia, not far from Blackwater. He also held the impressive distinction of being the youngest person ever to complete SEAL training, at the age of seventeen.

"From the time he was just a kid, he was just a miniature athlete. He was always very small for his age, so I think that really drove him to be the best, just because he was so much smaller than all the other children," said his mother, Katy Helvenston.

Like many of the private contractors Blackwater hired, Scott already had an accomplished military career by the time he came to work for the company. He had served as a Navy instructor, teaching high-altitude, low-opening parachuting tactics, before eventually leaving the military for opportunities in Hollywood. He took on some consulting work and helped Demi Moore prepare for her role in the movie *G.I. Jane.* But despite the highs, Helvenston found that the work wasn't bringing in a steady income, certainly not enough to support his young family. So the thirty-eight-year-old with incredible athletic skills looked for other options.

Helvenston had heard about high-paying jobs in Iraq for people with experience like his.

The downside was that most of the private companies doing the hiring were looking for a yearlong commitment, something he didn't want to sign up for because it would mean being away from his kids for too long. When he heard that Blackwater was offering contracts for just two months and paying around $600 a day, he was interested enough to apply.

Helvenston arrived at Blackwater's Moyock training facility in early March 2004. He spent ten days training in firearms and defensive driving before flying to Kuwait, a staging center for several contractors working for the U.S. government. From there, the plan was to go into Iraq, where he told his mother he would be assigned to the security detail guarding Paul Bremer. In addition to the Bremer contract, Blackwater protected a number of buildings used by the Coalition Provisional Authority in Iraq. The company had also just signed on as the subcontractor to provide security services for supply convoys. That would be Scott Helvenston's first and last mission for Blackwater.

JERRY ZOVKO didn't know Scott Helvenston before March 2004, yet both men hailed from a military background. Zovko, just thirty-one years old, had joined the Army after high school. He was assigned to the Eighty-second Airborne Division and had also worked as a military police officer.

Zovko, like Helvenston, left the military and looked for private work. He found it in Iraq, though not initially for Blackwater. Military Professional Resources Inc., better known as MPRI, had already established itself in Washington circles as a "go-to" destination for private solutions to difficult problems. The Alexandria, Virginia–based firm was started in the late 1980s by a retired Army general, and in the 1990s, the company offered the Pentagon an attractive solution for a delicate dilemma in the Balkans. The United States needed to be sure there would be a balance of power in Bosnia and Herzegovina if the region were to remain stable, yet the Clinton administration had vowed not to rearm the Bosnians. So the Bosnian government turned to MPRI to give it what it needed to defend itself.

Less than ten years later, the company that described itself as a "training, simulation, and government services company" found itself partnered with Kellogg Brown & Root and two other firms on a U.S. State Department contract training civilian police officers in emerging police forces around the world. For Jerry Zovko, that meant Iraq.

"That's why he went to Iraq, to train the Iraqis," said Jerry's mother, Donna Zovko. "He did not disclose to me that he would be carrying a gun and working for a company like Blackwater when he left. He was strictly going to a base to train Iraqis so that our young men could come home."

Zovko, like hundreds of other private contractors working in the country at the time, found another job when the MPRI work ended. In what would later become a common expression for contractors who left the military to work for private industry, Jerry Zovko was "going to Blackwater."

In early March, Erik Prince made a personal trip to Iraq to help pull together details on some upcoming contracts. Zovko was assigned to protect him. Prince was impressed with what he saw, including Zovko's near fluency in Arabic.

Toward the end of March 2004, Zovko called his mother, telling her he would be home for Easter. It was the last conversation she would have with him.

AT THE AGE OF THIRTY-EIGHT, Mike Teague had already served twelve years in the Army in places like Panama and Grenada, but it was in the rugged terrain of Afghanistan that he earned his Bronze Star. He had left the military years earlier and by early 2004 had joined Blackwater. Teague had left a low-paying security guard job in Tennessee and had gone to Iraq.

Wesley Batalona had spent some twenty years in the U.S. military, part of that time as an Army Ranger. His last tour concluded in Somalia, from which images of U.S. soldiers being dragged through the streets of Mogadishu had burned themselves into the international political psyche and had brought domestic pressure on the administration of President Bill Clinton to pull U.S. troops out of the area.

According to family members, Batalona had trouble finding a market for his skills in the civilian arena. He took a job as a security guard at an upscale tourist resort in his native Hawaii to make ends meet, but he had heard that contractors with experience were in demand in Iraq. He signed on to the same contract training Iraqis that Jerry Zovko did. The two would become colleagues and fast friends.

SCOTT HELVENSTON ARRIVED in Kuwait as part of a six-man team and immediately began making impressions on those he worked with, some of them good, some of them clearly strained. He was described by one coworker as a guy who bucked negativism and approached life with a "can do, damn glad to be here" attitude. But it was a rocky beginning for him with his new employer. He didn't get along with one of his supervisors, and the situation had him so upset that he wrote an e-mail shortly after arriving, addressing his concerns to the owner, president, and upper management of Blackwater.

> It is with deep regret and remorse that I send you this
> e-mail. During my short tenure here with Blackwater, I have
> witnessed and endured some extreme unprofessionalism.
> First, I would like to begin this e-mail with a few positive
> notes. My training began on March 1st. During my ten days
> of training I experienced some quality training conducted

by quality instructors. The British firearms instructor . . .
and even the hand to hand instructors displayed some very
skilled and professional instruction . . . others as well but
I am not in recollection of their names. Unfortunately
though I must explain to you there is an individual amongst
the ranks that has proven to be very manipulative, duplici-
tive [sic] . . . .

The e-mail went on to single out one person Helvenston believed was not up to the task at hand. It laid out his specific concerns for a mission he wasn't planning on.

Three days ago I was put on a team with two of the men who
came down from Baghdad. Cool . . . ready to go! Yesterday
that was changed. OK, things seem to be a bit disorganized
but I am still on it. We spent the last two days working,
out for meals, getting to know one another and in general
bonding. We have been told that we are scheduled to leave
two days from now to escort a bus up to Baghdad. Tonight I
went out with my new teammates for dinner and afterwards
my team leader took us out to a huhka bar. This is a non
alcoholic bar, it is a very dignified custom that the local
muslims partake in and was . . . well my first time doing
such a thing. At roughly 2200 hours this evening I receive
a call asking me if I can leave tomorrow 0500 with a new
team leader. God's honest truth . . . I am sitting there with a
fruit drink and a piece [sic] *pipe in my mouth (completely*
legal) feeling . . . well . . . dizzy as shit and a bit nasuated
[sic] *and my response was no. My bags were not packed and*
I just didn't feel up to it.

Ultimately, Helvenston agreed to go on the mission, and early in the morning of March 30, he and his new team set out in two Mitsubishi Pajeros, escorting flatbed trucks to pick up kitchen equipment from one location and deliver it to another. Their destination was on the far side of Fallujah, but they found that as the day wore on, they were running out of light. The decision was made to spend the night at Camp Fallujah, the military base just east of town.

March 31 started early for the four men and the convoy they were escorting. Their differences set aside for the time being, the men hopped into their Pajeros and pulled out, heading to the heart of Fallujah. Westerners would typically avoid the downtown area, opting instead for a bypass route around the city, but that morning, the convoy set out on Highway 10, right through the busy streets of the city. There were just two men per vehicle. Two of the men who would have provided rear cover in the vehicles had been held back to help with clerical work.

Helvenston and Teague were in one SUV, Batalona and Zovko in another, as the convoy drove a little over a mile into town. With traffic coming to a halt, the convoy found itself stuck in a growing swarm of traffic and people. Suddenly, a few armed men emerged from the streets and approached the vehicle that Helvenston and Teague were in. They fired off shots, hitting the Blackwater men in the back of the head, the stricken men's bodies slumping forward in their seats. Witnesses watched the other Pajero attempting to move out of the way, but it failed to pass through the gathering crowd fast enough. Within minutes of the first attack, Zovko and Batalona were also shot.

The crowd began working itself into a frenzy. Locals videotaped as a mob of men and boys began to chant and celebrate, many of them cheering, "Fallujah is the graveyard of Americans."

The video showed a chilling display of hatred, as the bodies were burned, ripped from the vehicles, beaten, and dragged through the streets to a steel bridge spanning the Euphrates River. The crowd was jubilant, chanting like football fans celebrating a Super Bowl victory. A torso, now decapitated, was tied with electrical cord and hung from the girders. A second body, blackened from the fire, was also strung up for the cheering crowd to see.

It was sometime between 3:30 and 4:30 in the morning in McLean, Virginia, when Erik Prince got the call. In Moyock, North Carolina, Gary Jackson had gotten word of the attack as well. Jackson headed into his office at the Blackwater training facility, where he was joined by Chris Taylor, who had just been promoted to vice president of strategic initiatives, and Mike Rush, the director of Blackwater Security Consulting. They linked up with Prince by phone, as he arrived at his unmarked office in a McLean high-rise in the dark hours of morning. The details were still sketchy, but they knew that four of their own had been killed.

"I'd been a low-level officer before, but I'd never had anybody under my responsibility seriously injured or killed," said Prince. "That struck home."

It wasn't long before the images began showing up on TV screens. The pictures shown on Arabic networks were incredibly disturbing: the chanting crowd, the burning vehicles, the bodies hanging from the bridge. Even what aired on American networks was disturbing, and those pictures were heavily edited.

"It was already on CNN," said Taylor. "We had preliminary information that it was our guys."

It was an outrage for Prince, remembering his trip to the area just weeks before. "The first thing I thought of when I saw that was Jerry [Zovko] would be the guy to go and sort this out and find the guys who did this," said Prince.

By midmorning, the worst was confirmed. The four men were four of their own. Prince, Jackson, Taylor, and Rush knew what they had to do. Jackson was angry but tried to keep his emotions in check.

"I was pissed; you know, I come from the Special Operations community, and I was mainly just pissed," said Jackson. "You've got to understand at that particular point in time, no matter how bad it was, it was going, and we had stuff to do."

The four dead men had listed next of kin information in the company paperwork. The four Blackwater executives packed their bags and headed out to inform the families. U.S. marshals or sheriff's deputies would be waiting at their respective destinations.

Prince set out for Cleveland to tell Jerry Zovko's parents. Jackson, who had seen Mike Teague less than two weeks before, would be the one to tell Teague's wife and fifteen-year-old son that Mike wouldn't be coming home. Taylor headed for a San Diego suburb to tell Tricia Irby, Scott Helvenston's ex-wife, that the father of her children had been killed. Rush was on a plane bound for Hawaii.

THAT AFTERNOON, Katy Helvenston was sitting in her home office in a bedroom community just outside Orlando, Florida, when images of the gruesome, chaotic mob scene flashed on her TV screen. She couldn't help but think briefly of the son she called Scotty.

"The original clip I saw was on CNN, and it was during the lunch hour," recalled Helvenston. She was working in real estate, preparing for a closing that afternoon, but the commotion on the television screen became harder and harder to avoid. "I heard this noise on the TV, and it kind of caught my attention, and I saw this body hanging from a bridge and this mob just going crazy, and I said, 'My God, when is this gonna end? This is insane.'"

Helvenston needed a break from the chaos, so she changed the channel but switched back a half hour later. That's when she heard the word that would come back to haunt her. Someone on the news had mentioned the men hanging from the girders were "contractors."

"I thought, oh, road construction or people working on the pipeline or something," said Helvenston. "Scotty wasn't even in, I mean, that was his first day in Iraq. I mean, he'd gone up from Kuwait City, had spent one night outside Baghdad."

She called her younger son, Jason, who assured her that Scott could take care of himself and that she was worrying too much. She packed up her paperwork and headed off to her closing, trying to put the images out of her mind. When she got home a few hours later, there were seventeen messages waiting for her, most of them from Jason.

"He kept saying, 'Mom, it's Blackwater, it's Blackwater,'" said Helvenston. The news had been trickling out in bits and pieces. There was still no word from the company as to whether Scotty was involved. Katy called Scotty's ex-wife, who had nothing more to add, so she got on the Internet and Googled Blackwater.

"There was an 800 number, so I called it and just told them that my name is Katy, and I was Scott, Scotty Helvenston's mom, and is he OK? And they just said they didn't know, and I said,

'How could you not know? I saw this on the TV six hours ago,'"
said Helvenston.

CHRIS TAYLOR WAS HEADED to San Diego to tell Scott's ex-
wife and the mother of their two children what had happened.
It was late by the time he arrived, close to midnight, but it didn't
matter; the images were already on television and had been circulating for half a day. A U.S. marshal was waiting for him at
the airport, and the two set off for Tricia's home. Taylor knocked
softly on the door. It took about a minute for him to explain that
there had been an attack on a convoy and that he had some bad
news to share. Scott's ex-wife collapsed on the ground outside
the door.

After Tricia came around, Taylor and the marshal helped her
into the house. Taylor stayed to talk with her for a little while,
asking if there was anyone he could call, anything he could do
for her. Before he left, he handed her a folder. Inside was information about the Defense Base Act. Established in 1941, the
act was originally created to provide insurance for contractors
working on military bases outside the United States. It was later
amended to help provide coverage for the vastly expanding roles
contractors were filling for the government.

After he left, Taylor made a call back to Moyock. Now that
Tricia had been informed, Blackwater could tell Scott's mother
the news she didn't want to hear.

DONNA ZOVKO skipped her morning coffee on March 31 and
headed to her family's automotive repair shop in Cleveland. She
wanted to get there early, mostly because she wanted to leave

early. Today was the day that she would pick up the DVD of
Brother Bear that she had ordered for her grandkids. She was looking forward to spending the afternoon watching it with them.

The last customer had left by noon. Donna had the radio on
in the background, and the news was reporting something terrible: four Americans killed in Iraq, their deaths celebrated by
the Iraqis, their bodies publicly displayed as a sign of victory. It
reminded her of what had happened to the American soldiers
in Somalia. She wrote her son Jerry an e-mail, urging him to be
extra careful. She asked for him to respond. An hour went by
with nothing, so she e-mailed him again, reminding him that the
next day was April Fools' Day, please be careful. With that, she
packed up her things and left the shop.

Her cell phone rang as she stood at the cash register at the
local drugstore. It was her husband asking her to come back to
the shop. Annoyed, she told him that she was spending the rest
of the day with the grandkids. She hung up. He called again and
told her a friend was at the shop, and they needed to tell her
something. She hung up again. The phone rang a third time.

"The third time, my husband couldn't hold it anymore," recalled Zovko. "He said Jerry had been killed." Donna dropped the
phone and fell to the ground. When she came to, she returned
to the shop.

A family friend had heard the news from his son, who also
worked for a private contractor. The friend wanted the Zovkos
to hear it from someone they knew rather than from a complete
stranger, so he had called Donna's husband. When Donna arrived at the shop, she was in a state of disbelief. There were so
many questions flying through her head. What company was it
that Jerry had worked for? She remembered that just days earlier,
a postcard had come to the house from the Department of Labor

stating that Jerry's benefits were changing because he was working for a new company in Iraq. The name of the company was on that postcard. Donna headed home. It didn't take long for her to find the card. The company was called Blackwater. By now, it was already around 5:00 p.m. Would anyone be there? She dialed the number.

"I called Blackwater, and they told me that they can't tell me anything, not right away, and to give them a call in a little bit," said Zovko.

She waited for a little bit and called again. She got the same woman on the other end of the phone.

"She said, 'Mrs. Zovko, I will be a person that you can speak to. One of the young men was your son, and if there's anything you need or anything I can do for you, you just call me at this number,'" recalled Zovko.

The voice at the other end of the line also told her someone from the company would be coming to the house. Donna gave her the address of the house where her son and daughter-in-law were living. By 7:45 p.m., the phone rang.

"They're here," Zovko heard her daughter-in-law say.

When Zovko and her husband arrived at her daughter-in-law's home, Erik Prince was already in the dining room. He had been accompanied by a sheriff's deputy, bringing the official word that Donna could no longer deny: her son was dead. Prince extended his arms. Her husband was struck by how much he thought the man before him looked like his own son.

"He told me about his family, he told me about his boys," recalled Donna Zovko. Prince told Donna that he had met Jerry, that he knew him, and that he believed if anyone would survive the war in Iraq, it would have been Jerry. Donna tried to take it all in between the tears. That's when Prince did something he doesn't normally do with strangers. He opened up about his own life, telling Zovko that he had lost his wife to cancer.

"I don't know if he had lost anyone before on the job, but I knew he knew what that was because he was living it, losing his partner and love of his life, and mother of his kids," said Zovko.

It wasn't long before Donna's extended family had gathered at the house. Prince extended his condolences once more and left a check for $3,000 to cover funeral expenses. He had given Donna his cell phone number and told her he would be back in nine days for Jerry's wake. There was something more that Donna wanted.

"I asked him to bring me the latest picture he had of my son," said Zovko.

KATY HELVENSTON HAD SPENT the better part of the evening on the phone with a young woman from Blackwater. To her it was just a voice, but it was the only connection she had to her son at that moment, and she wasn't about to let it go.

The voice told her that more than four hundred Blackwater employees in Iraq had been asked to check in, so Helvenston called every hour on the hour to see who had called and who had not. Scott had been so good about calling her every day, but today there had been no word from her son. As the hours crept from evening to night to early morning, Helvenston was told that the number of employees who had checked in was ticking up, but still no word from Scott. The company, of course, already knew that her son was one of the victims, but employees were sticking with the plan to notify Tricia first.

As it neared midnight in Florida, the woman on the other end of the line told Katy she was going home but that she would call her if she heard anything. She gave her another friendly voice to talk to, and that's exactly what Katy did.

"I just sat there and told them about Scotty's entire life," recalled Helvenston, from the time he was a little boy until the time he went to Blackwater. "I said, 'I want you to know my son.' And there was never a word on the other line, and a couple of times I would say, 'Are you still there?' and she would say, 'Yeah.'"

The call finally came around 3:00 a.m.

"She just said, 'Katy, he's gone,'" recounted Helvenston, "and I said, 'Will someone be here for me?' And she just said, 'No.' I said, 'My son was just slaughtered, and no one's gonna be here?' And she said, 'No one's gonna be there.'"

Gary Jackson had already arrived at Mike Teague's home to tell his wife that she was now a widow, and their fifteen-year-old son that he was now without a father. Jackson knew Mike Teague, and he knew how close he was to his son. Yet he was unprepared for just how hard Teague's death would hit his son.

THE VERSIONS of the Fallujah attack that aired on Arab news networks were far more detailed than the edited versions airing in the United States. The unedited versions showed close-up pictures of the bodies and generated outrage among many who saw them. White House spokesman Scott McClellan called the attack "despicable" and blamed it on those who were doing "everything they could to prevent the handover of power to a sovereign Iraqi government."

The reaction in Baghdad was somewhat different. Bremer was concerned that the attack drew attention to the fact that the coalition was not in control of Fallujah. General Sanchez tried his best to curb any emotional reaction. To him, the attack was just another tactical event in a theater of war.

According to Sanchez, "The fact that we had these four souls ambushed, killed, and then dragged through the streets and stuff was, from a military perspective and theater-strategic perspective, it was almost a, I won't say nonevent; it was very tragic obviously, but it was not something that was going to have a major effect on the military situation in the country."

Still, the decision was made: the Marines would lead an assault on Fallujah. Sanchez believed there were political considerations behind the decision. The handover of power was coming quickly, and a U.S. presidential election was just over seven months away, "and the implications are horrific," said Sanchez. "OK, so that's what drives the necessity for us to make a statement to the defamation."

The general unveiled an operation that had been shelved the previous fall, when the Iraqi interior minister had put a stop to it. It was a plan for U.S. troops to clean out Fallujah, and it would be messy, but Sanchez could see the benefit of seizing the opportunity.

"You have almost a convergence of interest between military and the political leadership because, from my perspective, even though the timing was absolutely wrong to advocate for an offensive, Fallujah was a safe haven," said Sanchez. "We had never gone in there and tried to really clear it out, and we'd been having problems there for months, so this becomes, for us, the military, and for me, probably a pretty good opportunity for us to go ahead and use this as a means to go in there and once and for all eliminate it as a safe haven."

But Sanchez knew it wouldn't be an easy operation. An estimated twenty thousand insurgents were living and operating among a civilian population numbering in the hundreds of thousands. Weeding them out would mean a lot of collateral damage. It was going to be a bloody mission.

Operation Vigilant Resolve was launched in the early days of April in Anbar Province. Traffic was controlled in and out of Fallujah, and General Sanchez's promise of a bloody battle proved true. But within days, it became evident that the political cost of securing Fallujah would be too high: too many civilians were being killed in the battle. Under pressure, the U.S. and coalition forces agreed to pull back to the outskirts of the city, leaving many with the feeling that the job still hadn't been finished.

BY APRIL 9, Blackwater confirmed publicly that it had launched an internal investigation into the Fallujah killings. Company vice president Patrick Toohey headed up the effort. He told the *New York Times* that early details indicated the four employees had been set up by men dressed as members of the Iraqi Civilian Defense Corps, and when the road ahead was blocked, armed men emerged from the crowd and attacked. The report itself was never made public, but it seemed a likely theory. Just weeks before, General John Abizaid had expressed his own concerns about infiltration of the Iraqi police forces to the Senate Armed Services Committee.

Blackwater was unprepared for the onslaught of media attention that followed the Fallujah incident. Erik Prince had spent years keeping out of the public eye. The handover of power from the Coalition Provisional Authority to the Iraqis was just months away, and the company's biggest client, the State Department, wasn't looking for any additional problems. Yet the images had generated media interest around the world.

People wanted to know more about Blackwater.

Prince's friend Paul Behrends was now working for the Alexander Strategy Group, one of Washington's top lobbying firms with deep ties to Republican power brokers. Prince hired Behrends to take on Blackwater as a client. Behrends knew the Fallujah attack posed a sticky problem for the company. While media outlets around the world wanted information, the State Department was equally insistent that none get out. It put Blackwater in a delicate balancing act.

"This company never sought any media attention, and when it did come after Fallujah, then we were kind of conflicted," said Behrends. "We weren't allowed to have a kind of normal outreach to the media."

The Fallujah incident wasn't directly connected to the State Department contract, but Blackwater executives understood the department's opposition to the company having a public face. Blackwater executives, nonetheless, felt they had no choice but to issue press releases and attempt to clarify statements in the press—the images of the four men killed in Fallujah were too stark to leave alone. The world wanted to know more about who these contractors were, and so did lawmakers. Within days of the Fallujah attack, Prince met privately with Republican lawmakers on the Hill to explain how the contracting business worked and how Blackwater played a role. He had been a huge financial supporter of Republican candidates in the past, a point not lost on Democrats. But Democratic leaders were also determined to get to the bottom of the contracting issue. They demanded that Secretary of Defense Donald Rumsfeld provide them with "an accurate tally" of the numbers of private security contractors operating in Iraq. Just how big had this "shadow army" gotten? Other prominent Democrats wanted the Pentagon to provide

written guidelines laying out the rules of engagement for contractors, and they wanted to know how contractors would coordinate their actions with both the U.S.-led coalition and the Iraqi
government. They were all questions that would eventually come
to a boiling point before they would be answered.

JUST DAYS AFTER the Fallujah attack, there was another incident involving Blackwater security guards, this time at the Coalition Provisional Authority building in Najaf. Like most incidents
in Iraq, there are always more than two sides to the story, but
the differing accounts between the company and the military
were dramatic and highlighted some of the growing frustrations
of commanders on the battlefield when it came to working with
private contractors.

A small Blackwater team had been assigned to protect the
building where the Coalition Provisional Authority operated in
Najaf. In early April, the building reportedly came under attack
by men believed to be members of an Iraqi militia.

The initial Blackwater account implied that hundreds of men
were attempting to overrun the building. The Blackwater employees took up positions on the rooftop and began firing, but
they were also videotaping as they took aim at people who could
not be seen on camera and fired off shots, one after the other into
the street below. A Marine on-site called in for help, saying that
the building was being overrun and that they were running dan-
gerously low on ammunition. Blackwater vice president Patrick
Toohey would later tell the *New York Times,* "They were down to
single digits of ammo, less than ten rounds a man." The Blackwater guards called Baghdad for help. Paul Bremer was told the
men were under attack and needed help right away. Blackwater

had three helicopters on the Bremer detail. He had a decision to make: let the military handle the incident, or allow the company-owned helicopters under contract to the State Department to resupply the men with ammunition and retrieve a wounded Marine. Bremer gave the order for the helicopters to go and help. But the Blackwater men also wanted to make sure it was OK with the boss.

"They called me, saying they had permission from Bremer to go and resupply them, but they wanted to know if it was OK with me, because they knew the helicopters were self-insured," said Prince, who told them to go.

General Sanchez saw the incident differently. In his book, *Wiser in Battle,* Sanchez recounts that his men started getting radio reports from a Marine at the Najaf location, saying that he and his men were under attack. Sanchez ordered close air support. When his pilots subsequently sent word that they had seen no sign of enemy activity, he was dismayed. Sanchez got the Marine, a major, back on the line, only to hear more of the same: there was "fighting everywhere. This may be the last radio call we can make before we get overrun. Send help."

For Sanchez, it didn't add up, so he went to see for himself. What he found on the roof was nothing more than occasional sniper fire. Sanchez informed the Marine major that he had not been under attack by hundreds of Iraqis, and that the information he was being told, reportedly by Blackwater guards, was not accurate.

Videos showing Blackwater contractors hunkered down on the roof would later make their way onto YouTube. What they showed was consistent with General Sanchez's account, and it was peppered with comments from the Blackwater guards that weren't going to help lessen the "cowboy image" the company had already earned in Iraq. The Blackwater men appeared to be overreaching, to say the least.

The friction between the Pentagon and the State Department over the use of private contractors in a war zone was intense. Sanchez didn't hold back on how he felt about it.

"The State Department doesn't have the capacity or the expertise to be able to supervise and operate a small militia; that's what these guys are, the ambassador's personal militia. Nobody would like to hear that term, but that's what it is," said Sanchez. To his way of thinking, using Blackwater for security for the ambassador and a few key people was acceptable, but on the whole, contractors were no substitute for using armed forces. Nonetheless, contracting was mushrooming into a billion-dollar operation, with no real oversight.

But Sanchez had another crisis to deal with that would eventually play a role in his leaving the military: the Abu Ghraib scandal. And although the scandal focused on the military personnel who ran the prison, there were private contractors involved as well.

ABU GHRAIB HAD long been known as a place of horror and fear. The prison, some twenty miles west of Baghdad, was notorious under Saddam Hussein. Prisoners were sent to Abu Ghraib, never to be heard from again. After the U.S. invasion, the facility was run as a U.S. Army detention center for Iraqi prisoners of war. Former CIA officer Bob Baer described conditions at the prison shortly after the Americans entered Iraq, in an interview with *CBS News*: "There were bodies that were eaten by dogs, torture. You know, electrodes coming out of the walls. It was an awful place."

Back in late 2003, news of more horrors had begun to trickle out, only this time, the prison was being run by the Americans. In November 2003, a prisoner had died during an interrogation. The Army had already begun an investigation and by March had removed some seventeen soldiers from duty pending charges of detainee abuse. In April 2004 the scandal blew wide open.

A *CBS News* program aired now famous photographs of Iraqi detainees in humiliating positions. They were photographs taken by their American captors showing naked Iraqi men, piled one on top of the other. One photograph showed a detainee with a hood draped over his head standing on a box with wires attached to his hands. Once the images were out in the public domain, the Army launched a damage control mission, telling reporters that the behavior of a few Americans was not representative of the U.S. military as a whole. Secretary of Defense Rumsfeld testified before Congress: "These events occurred on my watch . . . as Secretary of Defense, I am accountable for them and I take full responsibility." He would tell the committee that there were more photographs they hadn't seen yet, many more. When it was done, eleven U.S. soldiers would be convicted of crimes related to the scandal. But they didn't do it alone. Working alongside the soldiers were private contractors, hired to perform interrogations on detainees. For them, there was no court-martial. They were performing jobs normally carried out by U.S. military, but they were virtually unaccountable to anyone: not the military, not local laws.

Within months, some of the alleged victims of abuse at Abu Ghraib took the only avenue of accountability available to them: they filed a civil suit against two of the companies that hired the contractors, CACI International and Titan Corporation. Both companies had been hired by the U.S. government to provide interrogation services at the prison, despite an Army ban on the practice.

An Army report into the abuses at Abu Ghraib found that an interrogator supplied by CACI and a translator provided by Titan were either directly or indirectly tied to the abuses.

CACI called the allegations in the lawsuit "malicious" and "false." Nonetheless, the investigation highlighted confusion within the government itself over just who was in charge of the contract personnel.

ALL TOLD, BY May 2004, there were tens of thousands of private contractors working in Iraq. Nobody knows the exact number, in part because the Pentagon claimed it didn't keep any figures, and in part because of the complexities of the subcontracting system. There were enough of them that the military realized someone needed to be coordinating their movements. Naturally, they hired a contractor to coordinate the contractors.

Tim Spicer wasn't the most obvious choice for the job. The former British military officer had called himself "an unorthodox soldier" in his own autobiography, making the case for why the British government should rely on private soldiers for certain tasks. He preferred the term *private military contractor,* or PMC, to the traditional term *mercenary.* Spicer had worked for an organization known as Executive Outcomes in South Africa. The company, later banned by the South African government, offered military muscle all over the continent, for a price. He later worked for a company called Sandline, which nearly brought down a British foreign minister in what became known as the "Arms to Africa" affair.

Sandline International had imported weapons to Sierra Leone in an effort to restore the government of President Ahmed Kabbah after a coup. The only problem was that the import was in breach of a United Nations weapons embargo. Spicer insisted that the British Foreign Office knew of his plan, and the incident sparked an investigation by the House of Commons Foreign Affairs Committee and launched a debate over whether hiring a mercenary company to transport arms fell within the ethical guidelines of the British Foreign Office.

An inquiry in 1998 turned up no evidence that officials had encouraged the supply of weapons, but Spicer continued to insist that the British High Commissioner knew of the plan, and that he had done nothing wrong. As a result of the affair, the government put stricter regulations in place, requiring that no officials have contact with private military companies without express permission.

Spicer left Sandline and had formed—and then quit—two other companies before starting Aegis Defence Services around the time of the Iraq War. The company was barely a year old and was not on the State Department's list of recommended security companies when the Pentagon awarded Spicer a $293 million cost-plus contract to coordinate and manage the more than fifty private companies operating in Iraq in May 2004.

People who knew about Spicer's more colorful appearances in the headlines were dumbfounded at how the U.S. government would hire him for such a position. While the Pentagon refused comment on the matter, a former DoD official said the contracting offices were under intense pressure to meet the emerging demands as quickly as possible, and contractors were the only way they could do it.

"The people in the contracting office didn't know who Tim Spicer was," insisted the former official. In one sense, he was perfect for the job: if contractors are beholden to no one but their clients, who better to coordinate them than a contractor who knew the business from all sides, including the least savory?

BY JUNE 2004 the coalition was scrambling to put the last-minute details on a handover of power to Iraqi authorities. There were a lot of lawyers involved. Pat Kennedy knew that there would be a continued and critical State Department presence in the country. The State Department would need the contractors even after the handover of power, but allowing them to fall under Iraqi law could prove cumbersome. Kennedy knew the contractors would need legal protection.

"People realized as we moved forward because of the need for protective security, there had to be a framework put into place," recalled Kennedy. "There was no government of Iraq framework then because there was no government of Iraq, so the idea was to construct an interim framework that all the CPA orders exist until replaced."

The last thing Paul Bremer needed was a member of his security detail being arrested by Iraqi police for something done in the course of protecting him. It was still effectively a war zone, and the enemy operated among the local civilian population. Bremer and his team needed a framework that would exempt civilians contracted by the U.S. government from prosecution under Iraqi law. The lawyers' answer was Order 17, which offered immunity to coalition staff and contractors from Iraqi legal action. It would be in effect until the Iraqi government replaced it. And the Iraqi government had other, more important issues to worry about.

"When you have insurgents killing people, and you have the need to protect personnel, and this is American personnel," added Kennedy, "if there is a high degree of professionalism on the part of the contract security personnel, the impetus to make changes may not be there, given all the other issues that the government of Iraq was trying to address."

So at the end of June, with the handover of power, it was done. Order 17 was in place. Only one question remained: if the Iraqi government didn't have authority over the contractors, who did?

STILL NOT SATISFIED with the information that Blackwater had given her about her son's death in Fallujah months earlier, Katy Helvenston called up Erik Prince's office in October 2004.

"I told him I wanted a copy of the incident report, and I wanted a copy of Scotty's contract that he had signed with Blackwater, and he said, 'Why?' and I said, 'I want to know what happened; I have a right to know what happened.'"

Helvenston didn't get the answers she was looking for that day, but she did get an invitation from Blackwater shortly afterward to a memorial service to honor her son and the other Blackwater men killed in Fallujah.

Under a blue sky, the families of the four men gathered in a park surrounding a small lake next to the main building at Blackwater's Moyock campus. It was a calm, serene scene, with trees around the water and stones scattered about with the names of the fallen engraved on them.

"Erik Prince did come up and shake my hand," said Helvenston, "and I said, 'Sir, I need to talk with you,' and he said, 'Well, I can't do that right now,' and he went and shook other people's hands. I thought we would talk later, but we didn't, and that handshake was all I got from him."

There was plenty of food and alcohol for the occasion. Donna

Zovko also wanted a moment with Prince. She found it outside the main building.

"We were talking about how hard it is and about the memorial. He was going to give a speech. I liked the garden, and I asked him if I could come and visit Jerry's headstone. He said, 'Mrs. Zovko, anytime you want to, you are allowed to come.'"

But Donna Zovko also wanted answers. The families were invited into a conference room, where they asked the questions that had been nagging at them. Donna wanted a full accounting of the events that led up to her son's death. What were the names of the truck drivers who were in the convoy that day and had survived the attack? Where was Jerry's cell phone? Where was his bag? Donna remembered someone at the meeting telling her that the information was confidential and that if she wanted the details, she would have to sue.

Neither Gary Jackson nor Erik Prince was at that meeting, though they both say they don't believe the comment was ever made.

By EARLY 2005, Donna Zovko and Katy Helvenston were tired of waiting for the information they believed might never come. They joined with the families of Wesley Batalona and Mike Teague to file suit against Blackwater and two named employees in a wrongful death claim.

The official complaint filed with the court in January alleged that Helvenston, Zovko, Teague, and Batalona had been told they would operate in teams of no less than six men; that missions would be performed in armored vehicles; and that rear gunners in each vehicle would have a "heavy automatic weapon, such as a SAW Mach 46, which could fire up to 850 rounds per minute, allowing the gunner to fight off any attacks from the rear." None of these promises had been kept. The families believed that Blackwater had cut corners and that their loved ones paid the price with their lives.

CHAPTER 6

Private Air, Private Eye

BEHIND THE CONTROVERSIAL HEADLINES, Blackwater's business was fundamentally unaffected by Fallujah, and it continued a meteoric rise. Prince had acquired Aviation Worldwide Services in 2003, a private airline with a small fleet of planes, and Blackwater executives were relocating the company from Florida to the Moyock facility. It was now operating its flight services under the name Presidential Airways. The addition complemented Prince's strategic goal of providing one-stop shopping for customers. It also gave Blackwater an upper hand in its bid for contract work, since the company could provide not only manpower to the U.S. government, but planes and helicopters, and the pilots who could fly them anytime, anywhere. It was a strategy that would pay off, but it would also help put the company in prime position for yet another controversy.

In September 2004, the Department of Defense announced that Presidential Airways had won a nearly $35 million contract to provide fixed-wing short takeoff and landing aircraft for airlift support in and around Afghanistan, Uzbekistan, and Pakistan. The flights would ferry military supplies to allied forces.

Within two months, Presidential Airways wasn't just providing the U.S. military with a team of twin-engine CASA C-212s, but with the pilots to fly them as well, pilots who would ferry U.S. and allied military crews and supplies throughout the region on a daily basis.

On November 27, 2004, Blackwater Flight 61 set out from Afghanistan's Bagram Air Base to ferry three military passengers to the remote provincial capital of Farah. A National Transportation Safety Board (NTSB) report later showed that neither of the Presidential pilots had flown the route before. There were six men onboard—three civilian members of the Presidential Airways crew and their passengers, three U.S. soldiers: Lieutenant Colonel Michael McMahon, the commander of an Army aviation battalion, and Chief Warrant Officer Travis Grogan and Specialist Harley Miller, both members of McMahon's unit.

According to reports, the plane was carrying some 400 pounds of illuminated mortar rounds, and Grogan and Miller were already onboard when the plane began to taxi. McMahon flagged it down to hitch a ride back to his unit. For unknown reasons, several minutes into the flight, the pilots took a low-level run through a mountain canyon. It was a route they had never flown before, and while both pilots had extensive mountain-flying experience in the United States, they hadn't received similar training in Afghanistan. The flight recorder captured chatter among the crew that was more appropriate for Hollywood than the military: "I swear to God, they wouldn't pay me if they knew how much fun this was." "You're an X-wing fighter *Star Wars* man." "You're [expletive] right, this is fun."

Within minutes, the chatter changed. As the plane began to

climb, it was clear that the pilots were running out of room to maneuver. "Oh, God," said one of them. Shortly afterward, the plane slammed into the rugged Hindu Kush mountains of central Afghanistan. Local officials reported that parts of the plane scattered on top of a mountain range that rose some 16,600 feet into the sky. While at least one of the passengers survived the initial crash, he wouldn't last the three days it would take rescuers to reach him. The rescue effort was hindered in part because the pilots had taken an unknown path. It was eight months after the Fallujah incident. Blackwater's death toll was mounting. Like the Fallujah massacre, the Presidential Airways crash would eventually lead to a wrongful death lawsuit, and more charges of fatal corner cutting.

THE BIGGER THE COMPANY GREW, the more trouble it inevitably courted. Yet Prince was determined to grow faster than ever in 2005. The Iraq occupation was beset by an insurgency that demanded more and more security for U.S. and allied civilians and military men and women. The war on terror was making most of its headlines in Iraq and Afghanistan, yet there was action in many other locations around the world. Prince not only had his own personal fortune available to spend, he also had healthy profits. Blackwater was bringing in cash from its target systems manufacturing business. The security business was thriving with the State Department. It had expanded its Worldwide Personal Protective Services (WPPS) contract to include security services for the new, massive U.S. embassy being built in Baghdad, and in June 2005, Blackwater was brought on as one of three providers for that contract; DynCorp and Triple Canopy were the others. It was a lucrative deal for Blackwater, which, in combination with a task order to provide aviation support, would earn approximately $473 million a year. The other two contractors combined stood to make around $98 million per year. The contract was for one base year with the option to renew for four additional years. In addition, Prince was already well on his way toward building an impressive air fleet. Still, he had his sights set on bigger ventures. There were private corporations that desperately needed security, starting with intelligence. Prince needed an intelligence business to cater to that market and top executives with global contacts. For starters, he needed Cofer Black.

Months earlier, Black had gained a firsthand impression of the CIA's overcapacity when he maneuvered his car through the CIA's parking lot looking for an empty space. He was there for a retirement ceremony. The agency had grown enormously since 1974, when he started his career as an operative. Back then, there was an original compound building surrounded by little more than trees and hills. Now there was a big new shiny headquarters and what seemed like miles of parking lot. Black had stepped down as the head of the CIA's counterterrorism unit to accept an ambassador's position as coordinator for counterterrorism at the State Department in December 2002, but he still had a lot of friends at the agency, one of whom was retiring. As Black steered his way over to the VIP section of the lot, he explained to the guard that he was an ambassador; there must be some place for him to park in there. But even that proved to be a challenge. There were now a lot of VIPs at the agency, too. The guard let him in, but the spot Black eventually discovered was so small, he had to wedge his car in between two others, roll down the window, and squeeze his six-foot, three-inch frame out of the opening.

The expanding payroll at the agency was just the tip of the

iceberg. There had been other significant changes since Black's early days. Upwards of 70 percent of the U.S. intelligence budget was now being spent on private contractors, with no slowdown in sight. The business of contracting private workers to the government's various intelligence agencies was well on its way to becoming a $50 billion-a-year industry. Cofer Black was not yet part of that bonanza. But Black's new job at the State Department would present him with the opportunity to meet Erik Prince.

Black accepted an invitation by Blackwater to be a guest speaker at a dinner the company sponsored in May 2004. He talked about policy and planning for the State Department's Anti-terrorism Training Assistance Program, which was just one part of his portfolio at State. Giving that speech proved a smart bit of networking. Six months later, he would resign his post at the State Department, and in early February 2005, Prince stunned Washington by announcing that Black was taking the position of vice chairman with the company. Black's thirty years of experience and healthy international Rolodex were obvious assets. But Blackwater was not then known to be in the business of private intelligence. Logistics, security, and training were one thing. A private CIA was something else entirely.

Black had spent much of his time in the CIA overseas as a top U.S. spy. He served no fewer than six tours abroad. In the mid-1990s, he became the CIA's task force chief in the Near East and South Asia Division. In the late 1990s, he had moved to serving as the deputy chief of the agency's Latin America Division.

Black showed no reservations about turning it all in for a private sector job. "After thirty-plus years, of which twenty-eight were primarily as an operations officer overseas, followed by the State Department job, I thought that was a good contribution, and I decided to look in other areas where I could contribute as well as spend a little more time at home with my wife and my family," he said. Left unmentioned was his new salary, believed to be far greater than any he was paid during his decades as a civil servant.

Black's mission for Blackwater was to call on his contacts around the world and generate new business. He also formed a consulting firm, The Black Group, which operated under The Prince Group umbrella. The company's Web site targeted corporations as potential clients, offering "protection for travel to high threat locations, business intelligence, threat assessments, specialized investigations, and tools to detect biological/chemical threats." Part consulting firm, part general contractor, The Black Group was an experiment in attracting business to Black's unique set of skills.

Black's higher-profile position, though, was as point man for Blackwater, attending international conventions and selling the private sector as a solution to the world's problems. It was a role he embraced enthusiastically. "It's like a 7-Eleven; they're fast, a little bit expensive, but they meet the requirement," said Black of his new contractor colleagues.

He believed so much in the efficiency of his new world that he thought midranking government personnel should spend a two-year sabbatical in the private sector to fully understand the need to be lean and effective. He also came to believe Blackwater could go anywhere in the world and solve any challenge, even those that had stumped local governments.

NOT LONG AFTER Black joined Prince, the management team at Blackwater prepared for a royal visit. King Abdullah II of Jordan had heard about the training facility Blackwater was running in

Moyock and had sent some of the members of his own elite security team for training.

Jordan had supported the United States throughout the war on terror, and the king had been rewarded with millions of dollars to help train Jordan's intelligence service. The king had, in turn, used some of that money to hire Blackwater to train members of his royal guard.

As the graduation of his men approached, the king decided to see for himself what Blackwater was all about. He called on his old friend Robert Richer at the CIA to help set up the trip. Richer headed the agency's Near East Division and had formed a close relationship with the king during the time Richer served as the CIA's chief of station in Amman.

In the spring of 2005, the men were joined by an entourage from various U.S. agencies for the trip to Moyock. The group spent the day not only attending the graduation ceremony of the king's men, but also touring the ever-expanding facility. The king saw the shooting ranges with the patented target systems and even took a turn practicing his own skills on the range. He also saw the driving track and a prototype of a new armored vehicle Blackwater was working on that would deflect a roadside bomb. Over a leisurely lunch, the king expressed interest in developing a similar training facility in Jordan. Before he left, Blackwater executives presented him with two gifts: an M-4 machine gun and a pistol. While the day had been an important opportunity for Blackwater to cultivate goodwill, it was also another chance for Richer and Prince to cross paths. It wasn't the first time the pair had met, as Richer had played a heavy role in the U.S. war in Afghanistan, and Prince's company had provided guards for the CIA there, but it was an important reintroduction.

By the end of the year, Richer had grown restless with the

changes at the CIA under Director Porter Goss. He believed Goss's staff was making it very difficult to carry out the agency's basic mandate by adding layers of bureaucracy, and he was growing increasingly frustrated by what he described as the military taking over more and more of what had traditionally been the CIA's field of operations. Richer had a choice to make. "I could not, I would never be disloyal, so I either had to agree with how he was running the place, or I was contrary to the necessary discipline. So I left," explained Richer.

Richer—like Black before him—had a lot to offer the private sector. "I managed thousands of people, [had] the ability to interact with heads of state. I had an understanding of world events and an experience base most people don't have," said Richer. He also had close ties to the military, being a former Marine himself.

Prince had heard that Richer had already announced his intention to leave the agency, so he reached out through a friend to set up a lunch meeting. Richer was attracted to Blackwater's relatively short chain of command and Prince's seeming flexibility. "I had ten or twelve offers—and I had lunch with Erik," recalled Richer. "A couple of days later he asked me if I'd thought about coming to work for him."

Richer began as Blackwater's vice president of intelligence on the Monday after Thanksgiving 2005, just weeks after leaving the CIA. The man who was once responsible for leading the Clandestine Service's collection and operational efforts was bringing his extraordinary experience and contacts to Blackwater.

But he was leaving an agency that itself had become dependent on private contractors to get the job done. "I'll be honest with you, you can't tell, except for the color of the badge, green being contractor, blue being staff, you can't tell who they are. I've actually had people giving briefs and giving a course of action; it's a standard of the business," said Richer.

From the agency's point of view, hiring contractors had inherent advantages. While there were significant hurdles in place for firing a civil servant, firing a contractor who wasn't performing could be done immediately. "We call the contract holder and say this person's not performing, please remove him," said Richer, "and they remove him overnight. That's power."

So hiring out had become commonplace within the agency, yet Richer wasn't comfortable with it. It was one thing for contractors to take care of the parking lot or the cafeteria. It was another for them to analyze intelligence data. "I think contractors should be a point of last return, they should be the last resort, they should be there to fill a gap," he said. Now, he was working on the other side of the gap.

By hiring both Cofer Black and Robert Richer, Prince wasn't doing anything that other private agencies hadn't done. But with their hirings, he was taking part in a trend that was getting more attention at the highest levels of the CIA, both inside and outside the building. While high-level employees were making an exit, the building was filling up with contracted personnel taking on the jobs of traditional employees. Many of the contractors hired in the sixteen military and civilian agencies that make up the U.S. intelligence community were sitting side by side with government workers. The Office of the Director of National Intelligence—itself created to oversee U.S. intelligence after 9/11—decided to conduct a survey on the use of contractors to see just how extensive the practice of hiring them had become. While Dr. Ronald Sanders, the human capital director for the Office of the Director of National Intelligence, wouldn't release the report (it was classified), he did say that some 40 percent of contract intelligence officers had been hired since 9/11 to collect or analyze data.

Sanders told the tale of an intelligence community gutted in the 1990s, causing agencies to lose core capability in some cases by as much as 40 percent. Budgets were tightened, priorities changed. So did the entire intelligence landscape. "I think it was just death by a thousand pinpricks," said Sanders. Soon the agencies weren't just hiring private contractors; they were losing personnel to them.

Concerns over a revolving door between the CIA and private contractors like Blackwater eventually reached CIA Director Michael Hayden, who had succeeded Goss after the latter's stormy eighteen-month tenure. It seemed too easy for highly trained civil servants to walk out the door with years of knowledge and experience and earn substantially higher salaries for contractors doing the exact same kind of secret work. The director created a study group to look at the problem and try to come up with a management strategy that was consistent with the agency's mission.

On May 30, 2007, Hayden said publicly, "We do not simply appreciate their skill and expertise—we rely on it." Yet he also admitted that the agency had not efficiently managed its contractor workforce. He wanted to explore reducing the agency's dependence on contractors by 10 percent, and wanted a review of which positions should be staff positions instead of being hired out. Hayden was also looking to beef up oversight of the contracting process at the CIA and look at whether a performance-based model would be more effective for some contracts. He didn't want the agency to become a "farm team for contractors." He was considering a new mandate that CIA employees who left the agency before reaching retirement age would have to wait eighteen months before going to work for a contractor.

None of Director Hayden's measures would affect Cofer Black and Robert Richer, both of whom had already left the agency and gone to work for Erik Prince. In February 2006, Prince announced the creation of a company to market intelligence skills to Fortune 1,000 companies doing business around the world. Total Intelligence Solutions Inc. was the result of merging The Black Group, Blackwater's Terrorism Research Center, and Technical Defense, an international strategy group. The new company would be headed by Black, who filled the role of chairman, and Richer, who moved from his position of vice president of intelligence for Blackwater to chief executive officer for Total Intelligence Solutions. The company was selling intelligence around the world. Much of it, because of modern technology, could be culled from open records, if you knew where to look.

While Black and Richer would maintain their offices at The Prince Group headquarters in Langley, another CIA veteran would help oversee the day-to-day operations of the new company headquarters located nearby in Arlington, Virginia. It was one of Black's old friends from his days at the agency, Enrique Prado. Total Intel boasted a team of employees who had experience in the CIA, Defense Intelligence Agency, Department of State, FBI, and Drug Enforcement Agency. Prince's idea was to provide one-stop shopping for the intelligence industry in much the same way Blackwater had done for the security and training business. Total Intel would offer such services as evaluating risk, technical and IT security, and consulting on issues like homeland security. Its Global Fusion Center was staffed around the clock, monitoring Web sites and gathering information available via open records. While the company didn't want to divulge its clients, it did post referrals on its Web site, though even they were vague. One quote was attributed to an unnamed senior intelligence community counterterrorism official at U.S. Special Operations Command: "I review [their intel] daily to ensure SOCOM is seeing what's hot. . . ." Like its Blackwater cousin, Total Intel offered a range of training classes on everything from intelligence, to operations, to what to do in a crisis. The company's employees, many of them coming from Blackwater, had already trained military, intelligence, and law enforcement personnel. But the company also offered security services for events and venues. Some of its clients were hedge funds, banks, and even cruise lines looking for security information in ports of call around the world. If there were a particular security threat in a tourist destination, a cruise line might simply change its port of call. This was the Cadillac of rent-a-cop agencies; this was a service backed by elite American intelligence. But it was a luxury service where demand would ebb and flow with the economy. Nonetheless, Total Intel was catering to the intelligence marketplace, the way that Blackwater had catered to the law enforcement and military markets.

THE CREATION OF TOTAL INTEL followed years of Prince and Jackson looking to expand the business in several directions at once. In addition to the growing number of security contracts and the expanding aviation projects, they put themselves forward for a stunning range of work once handled by government employees. In May 2005 Gary Jackson appeared before the House Homeland Security Subcommittee on Management, Integration, and Oversight to propose Blackwater for America's borders. Blackwater had turned its sights southward, and Jackson was offering testimony on how he thought security along the U.S.–Mexico border could be improved.

Jackson recounted the lessons the U.S. Navy had tragically learned with the USS *Cole* incident and the stunning lack of training the bombing exposed. He pitched the idea of "one-stop shopping" at the Blackwater complex, which had now grown to more than 6,000 acres: "While there are other companies out there who offer one or two distinct training services, none of them offer all of our services, and certainly not at one location."

Jackson told the committee that for $40,000 per person, Blackwater could train border patrol agents in an eighteen-week course that included tactical driving instruction, firearms, and classroom training. Added Jackson, "We believe it would take us approximately one year to train all two thousand agents." Jackson drew upon one of Prince's favorite comparisons, telling the committee, "Just as the private sector has responded in moving mail and packages around the world in a more efficient manner, so too can Blackwater respond to the emergent and compelling training needs."

It was around the same time that Prince incorporated Greystone Ltd. in Barbados. It was a sister company to Blackwater, a firm he would later describe as an international employment agency. While Blackwater would be Prince's company serving U.S. government clients, Greystone would cater to foreign governments and foreign commercial businesses. The company would focus on training programs and logistical support for governments other than the United States. It would also recruit third-country nationals from various countries to work on U.S. government contracts.

Oftentimes when Blackwater dealt with the State Department, the contract language was written to specify whether a position had to be filled by an American with a specific level of clearance or by a third-country national. "It's the affordability provision," said Prince. "I mean, you can't get an American to be a paid guard or a static guard at some of these locations for $20 or $30 a day; you just can't." Greystone boasted on its Web site of focusing "on providing stability to locations experiencing turmoil whether caused by armed conflict, epidemics, or natural or man-made disasters." The new company also promised "the ability to quickly and efficiently deploy anywhere in the world to create a more secure environment for our customers." Greystone would offer other countries and foreign-owned commercial operations the ability to facilitate large-scale stability operations that re-quired large numbers of people. The company immediately drew fire from Blackwater critics. It was being widely reported by some magazines and blogs that Greystone was drawing its employees from countries like Chile, Colombia, El Salvador, the Philip-pines, Fiji, and Croatia. The company refused to respond clearly, saying it wouldn't comment on where it found its third-country nationals, due to operational security concerns. But Prince did admit to drawing some contractors from Chile.

Bloggers had insisted that Prince's company had hired Chil-eans who had served under the brutal regime of Chilean dictator Augusto Pinochet. Prince denied the allegation and insisted there was a vetting process in place that included working through the U.S. embassy in the contractor's country of origin to conduct a background check on every employee. Prince insisted that the Chileans he had hired would have been in high school when Pinochet was in power.

Regardless of the Chilean controversy, drawing trained indi-viduals from third countries was a cost-saving measure that the U.S. government was OK with. If a foreign country needed se-curity teams, for example, Greystone might supply the low-level static guards. "This static guard position can be a local national or a third-country national," Prince explained. "Sometimes they'll say this has to be a third-country national, not a local national."

To run Greystone, Prince called on another former SEAL buddy. Chris Burgess had left the Navy in 1998 and headed for Montana, where he joined a ski patrol team. He tried his hand at racing before taking a more traditional job with a telecommunications company, and soon thereafter, he decided to go to business school. All along the way, however, his Blackwater friends kept calling. Bill Mathews reached out to Burgess, but Burgess turned him down. He had left the military behind and wanted to do something else with his life. Mathews was not to be deterred. "He kept bugging me; he'd give me a call every month or something like that until finally I'm like, OK, OK, OK," recalled Burgess, who decided to stop by Moyock for a visit in 2004 and check it out.

"Basically, Erik sat down with me and said, 'Hey, I have this entity, and the person who was in charge of it is no longer here, and I need someone to run it. Would that be something that would interest you?'" recounted Burgess. The answer was yes.

Burgess joined Blackwater, working at Moyock, overseeing its foreign affiliates. Eventually, he managed Greystone; Salamis, an aviation holding company that buys and leases aircraft to commercial customers and governments overseas; and an Iraqi-based company called al-Zalama, which provides static security personnel. With Greystone in particular, international business looked promising. "For a lot of those countries, money is not really an object," said Burgess. "They have the capital to get the training they want, and they're used to doing that, they're used to hiring expats to provide training for their troops, so it's not unusual."

Blending ex-military men from so many nations wasn't difficult. "There are a lot of guys who were in the military, and so we all have the same mind-set, have the same 'get it done' concept, which you don't see in corporate America in the way you interact with people or the way you think about a problem," said Burgess. "On the other hand, it's a business, so you think from a business perspective, which you don't have in the military at all; so it's this fascinating hybrid between the military and corporate America, which makes it so interesting."

Critics continued to worry about the lack of accountability for the private contracting industry, and for Blackwater in particular. Few critics paid much attention to Greystone and the other foreign affiliates—where the potential for abuse was perhaps much greater. Hiring foreign nationals, and working for foreign governments, let alone private corporations, gave Prince's companies a lot of latitude. Contractors can be fired, of course, but there is often not much other recourse for misbehavior.

In June 2005 a Blackwater guard shot and killed an Iraqi man, a father of six, along the side of a road in Hilla. At first glance, it was just another in a troubling series of shootings of Iraqi civilians by Western contractors, incidents that happened when the civilians approached too close to protected convoys. But this time, the contractors didn't even report the incident. The victim's family complained, and internal State Department e-mails suggested a cover-up.

Soon thereafter, Aegis, the company charged with coordinating contractor communications in Iraq and owned by Tim Spicer, had its own bout of trouble with shooting at vehicles when what became known as the "Trophy Video" was posted to the Internet. The video showed men in a convoy vehicle shooting from the rear at oncoming traffic and cars swerving to get out of the way. Someone proceeded to string a series of such videos together and set them to Elvis Presley's "Mystery Train" as some kind of trophy. Human rights groups were outraged, saying the video highlighted the problems with hiring mercenaries in Iraq.

The U.S. Army, which had hired Aegis, launched an investigation and concluded that no criminal charges were warranted. But the world had gotten an unsavory look at the hired hands working in a war zone far from home.

MOTHER NATURE PRESENTED Blackwater with an opportunity for better PR in August 2005. The Federal Emergency Management Agency (FEMA) described Hurricane Katrina as the single most catastrophic natural disaster in history, but what followed could only be described as one of the most catastrophic man-made disasters in American history. By now the stories are well known: A hospital had to stop its evacuation of patients because of sniper fire. A health care corporation had to hire a fleet of helicopters to get patients out. An ambulance company reported that shots were fired as Army vehicles tried to evacuate people who had been displaced from their homes. Louisiana's governor, Kathleen Blanco, mobilized some forty thousand National Guard troops to restore order and help with the relief effort. The Pentagon sent fifty helicopters to fly in emergency meals and water. It also sent eight civilian swift-water rescue teams and moved a hospital ship to the region.

As news of the approaching storm made headlines, Erik Prince wondered what he could contribute. Prince's company was just then taking delivery of a Puma, a medium-sized helicopter designed to fly in all climates, day or night.

"I remember calling and hearing on the news the levees breaking and people on the roofs," recalled Prince. "I called our aviation guys, and I asked when do those pilots get in because they were literally driving the Puma to Florida, they were ferrying it down there."

The pilots arrived at eight o'clock that night. Prince left instructions to let them rest, but as soon as they could, to get them in the air headed for Louisiana. He didn't have a contract, didn't have a customer, didn't have a mission. He told the pilots to get in the air; he'd figure something out before they landed. Prince's company had done a lot of training for the Coast Guard, and he called contacts there to offer his assistance. He also reached out to the National Guard, the state of Louisiana, and the Louisiana State Mariner Management Agency.

"Hey, we've got a helicopter, we've got a crew," Prince remembered saying. "Tell us where to go, what to do; we'll come and help."

Blackwater attached itself to the Coast Guard and ended up assisting in evacuation and relief efforts. The company posted news of its involvement on its Web site. That's when the private sector started calling to ask for Blackwater personnel on the ground as well. "Because there was a meltdown," recalled Prince, "the civilian law enforcement was scattered, and they'd taken losses as well, so we surged 145 guys in a couple of days, and they did private security, static security for some key infrastructure."

What seemed to begin as altruism had turned into yet another business opportunity.

The company searched its database of tens of thousands of resumés, looking to see who had the skills needed in New Orleans. There were lots of former law enforcement people on call, and most of the equipment that would be needed was already sitting on the shelf in Moyock. Company administrators managed to license the contractors as employees of an investigative security organization. A copy of that license was laminated and sent with each contractor, along with a copy of the standard Department of Justice use of force continuum for armed guards. The use of force continuum was a set of standard guidelines among law enforcement and military personnel detailing when it was appropriate to use escalating amounts of force.

Private companies started calling. Bill Mathews faxed contracts out as fast as he could. Blackwater guards almost immediately began patrolling a commercial facility for a major retailer, an oil and gas pipeline, cell phone infrastructure, hotels, and insurance companies.

As a sign of how low Blackwater's public image had sunk, there was a healthy dose of negative press even for this work in disaster-struck New Orleans. The thought of armed Blackwater guards on the streets of an American city rattled some nerves. Blogs reported that Blackwater guards were patrolling the streets almost indiscriminately, armed to the teeth. It was another exercise in frustration with the media for both Jackson and Prince, who believed that the stories were filled with inaccuracies.

"We were not patrolling the streets, our guys did not have arrest authority," said Prince. Jackson insisted that media reports of Blackwater guards taking people out of their homes were complete fabrications. "The reporters, they started that and they got it out there, and it was absolute falsehood," said Jackson, "downright lies, because it sold."

But the Blackwater guards did carry weapons, including long guns. The company also sent body armor to its pilots because of the reports of snipers shooting at helicopters.

"When our guys got to the French Quarter, there were bodies in the streets, not from the storm, but from looters that had beaten people to death, and we went and in some cases protected people at a hotel, and when they showed up at the hotel, the looters who were breaking windows in the Brooks Brothers across the street left. We didn't arrest them, we didn't shoot them, we didn't beat them," said Prince. Prince believed the presence of his heavily armed guards was deterrent enough and said that as the violence subsided, so did the public posture of his men, adding that within two or three days the body armor and long guns were gone, replaced by polo shirts and side arms.

In the worst of the aftermath, wealthy private citizens started calling, too. Prince recounts how one family lost contact with a branch of their extended family living on the Alabama coast, so they hired Blackwater to go and find them. Company personnel loaded an ATV and a trailer with a generator, food, water, and a satellite phone in the back of one of their CASA aircraft. The men sent out for the job knew that bridges were down, but there was a runway open about eight miles away from the house in question. They offloaded the supplies, strapped them to the trailer attached to the ATV, and headed out. When they knocked on the door, they told the residents that their relatives had been worried about them and handed them a satellite phone.

While the Katrina experience prompted new ideas for just what the security company could provide, it wasn't the kind of business Prince felt that he could take to the bank. "That kind of business is based on disaster, so you can't really build a business sitting around waiting for a disaster to happen," said Prince.

Nonetheless, the company would go on to contract with some states, like California, for disaster relief services.

BLACKWATER'S IMAGE in New Orleans wasn't something Prince was too worried about. He had never worried much about Blackwater's image—he preferred to stay quiet instead of launching a PR campaign to win over critics. The critics weren't the ones paying him, and his clients preferred Blackwater to be stealthy. Prince had more immediate battles to fight anyway. The Fallujah and Afghanistan lawsuits posed serious threats to the longevity of the company, and Prince needed more expertise in leading the litigation. This time, he went through a headhunter to find it.

Joe Schmitz had been the Pentagon's chief inspector general since 2002, with a powerful mandate to prevent waste, fraud, and abuse inside the Department of Defense. He had managed a staff of some 1,250 officers and employees; his work had included a comprehensive investigation of a $20 billion Air Force plan to lease airplanes from Boeing.

His report found that the deal was severely flawed, and that Air Force officials failed to gather enough information to be sure they were getting a fair price. Schmitz recommended major changes to the Air Force's procurement process. The Air Force blasted the report, saying it "non-concurs emphatically" with the conclusions.

But there was more than one headline in the case. In what would be an unofficial lesson for procurement officers, it was revealed that a Pentagon official involved in the negotiations had been in touch with a senior Boeing official about a job at the company. The Air Force eventually canceled the leasing arrangement amid allegations of improper collusion. The top Pentagon procurement officer and a Boeing official were sent to prison. Schmitz found himself the subject of questioning by the Republican senator from Iowa, Charles Grassley, chairman of the Senate Finance Committee. Grassley wanted to know whether Schmitz had blocked investigations into senior Bush administration officials in relation to the tanker investigation. To accommodate White House concerns about executive privilege, Schmitz had redacted the final report on the tanker deal before sending it to Congress. By the time it reached the Hill, names of administration officials—who may have pushed for the deal— had been blacked out. It meant they couldn't be investigated, if Congress didn't know who they were. Schmitz's office denied any wrongdoing. Nonetheless, he announced his resignation in the fall of 2005.

Before his stint as inspector general, Schmitz had spent much of his professional career in the private sector practicing law. He had also joined the Naval Reserve. Blackwater seemed a natural fit. "I wasn't really looking to become a general counsel or even a lawyer, but someone shortly after the Air Force scandals testimony said he had read the description for the general counsel position, so I called Erik and told him I wasn't interested in being general counsel, but I was intrigued by his company," said Schmitz.

Prince extended an invitation for breakfast and shared with Schmitz his greatest fear. "He reiterated his background to me and said he would face al-Qaeda anytime, but trial lawyers scared the shit out of him," said Schmitz. The Fallujah and Afghanistan suits loomed large. "Erik hired me to deal with these two litigation issues," he said.

By the beginning of August, he had a formal offer from Prince to become the general counsel and chief operating officer of The Prince Group. Schmitz had a conversation with then secretary of defense Donald Rumsfeld to negotiate his exit. Schmitz resigned in September and joined Prince at his headquarters in an unmarked McLean, Virginia, high-rise.

Among his first responsibilities as COO was helping Prince recruit a chaplain. "When people we deploy get killed or injured,

we have the same challenges the military does, so to have a chaplain of the Marine Corps who knew how to work with people
who dealt with what we dealt with on a personal basis was key,"
said Schmitz. They settled on two chaplains, one residing full-
time in Moyock, the other commuting down once a week, then
back to his home parish in West Virginia.

But prayers wouldn't help Blackwater or Prince's Presidential Airways in court. The Fallujah case had been bounced from
one court to another, and it wasn't going well. Prince made the
decision to countersue the attorney representing the estate of
the dead men for $10 million. Blackwater argued that the attor-
ney had aided in breaching the men's original contracts by suing.
Another attorney representing the families called the claim "ap-
palling." Prince insisted that the families themselves faced zero
exposure in the countersuit.

Blackwater also reached out to a law firm employing Ken-
neth W. Starr, the independent counsel who led impeachment
proceedings against former president Bill Clinton. It made for
a frenzy of headlines and became a popular topic of bloggers
now watching the company's every move. Prince's deep financial
backing of Republicans had already fueled conspiracy theorists
who now saw the hiring of Starr as deeply evil. "I never met him,"
Prince said of Starr, noting he only hired the firm "to prepare
a very narrow legal appellate argument that we were trying to
make."

Still, there was little denying Prince's preference for lawyers
affiliated with Republicans. The first legal team Prince hired to
handle the case included Fred Fielding, who not only had worked
in the Nixon and Reagan administrations, but also had been
a part of President Bush's transition team. Fielding later
took a position inside the George W. Bush White House.

With Joe Schmitz now running Blackwater's legal team, Prince resolved to continue to fight vigorously against both the Fallujah and Afghanistan lawsuits. An Army investigation had found that Presidential Airways was at fault in the November 2004 plane crash in Afghanistan that killed three employees and three U.S. soldiers. The inquiry found that Prince's company had broken its own rules by staffing the plane with crew members who were new to the region. The report went on to cite deficiencies in the company's training and flight planning. It was enough to prompt a lawyer for the families who had filed suit against the company to file an amended complaint, asking for punitive damages. The Afghanistan suit claimed negligence on the part of the company, saying the pilots were new to the region and had never flown the route they took the day of the crash. The suit also claimed the pilots failed to file a flight plan and strayed from the normal route. The attorney for the plaintiffs, Robert Spohrer, claimed the company cut corners, adding, "We cannot allow corporations to put their profits ahead of the safety of our men and women in uniform." But Presidential Airways couldn't afford to be found guilty of negligence, either. Not only would a decision against it be costly, but it would also set a precedent for the industry and increase the financial risk of other companies wanting to get involved in the contracting business.

Joe Schmitz faced an uphill battle in both the Afghanistan and Fallujah cases. The costs of Prince's expanding businesses were getting higher, on the ground, in court, and around the world.

In September 2005 Prince purchased more than 400 additional acres of land in Camden County, North Carolina, and went public with plans to build what would become the county's largest building, a more than 66,500-square-foot facility that would serve as the company's new headquarters. It was a big increase from the company's current office, the "lodge," at just 9,000 square feet. Blackwater also wanted part of its land to be rezoned to allow for an airport on-site. It would make it far easier for Prince to fly directly from just outside D.C. to Moyock.

Meanwhile, Cofer Black traveled around the world to drum up more business. Black had never really had to worry about what he said as a spy. Most of what he did was off the radar, out of the media glare. But now he was working for a company that was very much—despite its reluctance—positioned in the center of it. In March 2006 Black went to Amman to attend a trade show sponsored by the Jordanian government. Jordan had begun hosting the Special Operations Forces Exhibition and Conference as an annual event in large part because King Abdullah II believed that special forces were crucial to addressing the world's unfolding military challenges, and he was determined that Jordan, a key U.S. ally, remain on the cutting edge of training and equipment. SOFEX was an opportunity for companies in the counterterrorism and homeland security industries, not to mention the makers of specialized weapons equipment, to show their wares to world leaders and others who had money to spend. The live demonstration range and impressive list of guest speakers also provided an attractive lure for journalists from around the world.

Black arrived in Amman ready to pitch his company's products. He wasn't only pitching Prince's manufacturing or security capabilities; he was offering Blackwater as a brigade-sized force for hire for places like Darfur. "It's an intriguing, good idea from a practical standpoint," Black was quoted as saying, "because we're low-cost and fast . . . the issue is who's going to let us play on their team?"

Reporters and bloggers ran with it. The idea of Blackwater hiring itself out to anyone who could pay was irresistible, and the comments generated headlines and questions all over the globe. Would Blackwater work for dictators? Drug lords? Opposing governments? Black had no idea his comments would have such legs and would later explain that he was just trying to convey that Blackwater had the potential to bring together a brigade-like unit composed primarily of caregivers and nongovernmental organization (NGO)–type personnel, and that it would serve as its own security, creating a stand-alone unit to save lives. He probably really meant: Blackwater already had military muscle, so why not add a do-gooder component?

"I made the rounds of African countries and ambassadors and heads of state," he later said, "and I never heard anyone say it's a bad idea." But the question of political accountability was left hanging.

A year before Black's comments in Amman, Erik Prince had proposed similar ideas. At a speaking engagement sponsored by the National Defense Industrial Association on special operations and low-intensity conflict, Prince made his pitch for what his company could do in places like Darfur.

"In areas where the UN is, where there's a lot of instability, sending a big, large-footprint conventional force is politically unpalatable; it's expensive, diplomatically difficult as well," said Prince. "We could put together a multinational, professional force, supply it, manage it, lead it, and put it under UN or NATO or U.S. control, however it would best be done; we can help stabilize the situation."

Prince envisioned a quick reaction force that would attach itself to NGOs operating in volatile regions, providing security that he referred to as "relief with teeth." If NGOs were engaged by Janjaweed militia in Sudan, for example, then his security units would fight back. He believed his company could do it with far fewer men than the international community had been proposing. He envisioned a relief team in which "everybody carries guns, just like Jeremiah rebuilding the temple in Israel—a sword in one hand and a trowel in the other."

For Prince, it all seemed so simple: just run your army, or NGO, like a business (and, conversely, run your business like the military). "Make sure the vehicles have fuel, and the oil's been changed and the tires inflated, batteries in the radios, and that they have a common frequency and a medevac plan and patrolling and put out a very simple early warning network. Sprinkle a couple hundred Thuraya [satellite] phones across [Darfur], and when that local village, the chief, is getting attacked . . . you call with a Thuraya phone; there's an embedded GPS, so immediately they call into an operations center, and you're gonna know exactly where they're calling from," he explained.

Just months after Black's comments made their way around the globe, Prince himself was on his way to Darfur. Months earlier, Blackwater's vice president for strategic initiatives, Chris Taylor, had received a personal invitation he couldn't refuse. He had gotten a letter from the president of Southern Sudan. "We were reached out to by the U.S. government and by the president of Southern Sudan for some help," said Taylor.

Blackwater was asked to help provide training for the president's personal security detail, so Taylor made the first of several trips to the area to get a handle on what was needed and try to figure out how Blackwater could fill the gap.

Within a year he returned with Erik Prince. In June 2006, the pair visited a refugee camp with a local NGO. After it landed on a dirt runway, refugees enthusiastically greeted the plane, helping to unload supplies and take them to a distribution hut.

The team also visited with tribal elders and recorded the encounters. They wanted to hear for themselves what was going on. At first, said Taylor, only the men would speak. "We got to the final hut, and these three or four women let loose and said what we need is security, nobody will protect us. Everybody has forgotten about us," he recounted.

At the end of the day, as the men boarded their plane to fly out, Prince turned to Taylor. "We need to help these people," he said. Their exit was hampered as the Russian plane got stuck on the muddy runway. "Two hundred to 300 refugees came to help dig the plane out," recalled Taylor. "They were singing songs and yelling and screaming and having a good time." It painted a surreal picture for Taylor at the end of an eventful day.

Prince was convinced that while the international community had done far too little to resolve the killing of innocents, his own men could have an immediate impact. "If the Janjaweed had their knuckles rapped hard a couple of times in the process of killing and attacking innocent people, if they got corrected a few times, they would figure out that's not a policy they could continue to make," he said later.

Could Blackwater do what Cofer Black had boasted and help save Darfur?

The Bush administration had placed sanctions on what a private company could and couldn't do there. If Blackwater was to participate by providing security for NGOs or anyone else in the region, it would have to be with the approval of the U.S. government, and Prince's men would have to be armed with a Technical Assistance Agreement (TAA). A TAA allows a U.S.-owned company to discuss and share technical data with a non-U.S. entity. It is a safety measure set by the Department of State in an effort to keep a handle on what kinds of services and information U.S. companies share overseas. Taylor knew the company couldn't operate in the region without one, so he took the letter he had received from the president of Southern Sudan, Salva Kiir Mayardit, and stuffed it in a FedEx pouch, along with a letter from the company requesting a waiver, and shipped it to the White House. The letter went unanswered. Taylor assumed the Bush administration had its own plans for Darfur, but nobody ever told him anything conclusive.

PRINCE'S COMPANIES had experienced phenomenal growth in large part based on U.S. government contracts. But the company—not solely a defense service provider, but with private clients as well—faced a precarious dilemma when it came to its public image. Its largest client preferred Blackwater remain low profile. That would have been OK with Prince, but it didn't take into account what would happen if the company itself came under continued and rapid fire.

CHAPTER 7

Under the Gun

TAKING A PAGE from his businessman father, Prince was investing his money heavily in research and development at Blackwater. He wanted to expand the company's air force, and not simply by buying more planes. This time, he wanted to build his own, so he commissioned a team that started development on the Blackwater airship. The blimp-type craft was assembled in a hangar, just a few minutes' flight from the Moyock facility. The 120-foot-long airship was built to fly between 5,000 and 10,000 feet, unmanned. Prince was hoping to lease it to the U.S. government for jobs like taking aerial images of border areas and then sending them to the appropriate agencies, or taking aerial images of trouble spots like the now infamous "Airport Road" that connected Baghdad's airport to the Green Zone. Insurgents had been planting roadside bombs along the route that were killing soldiers and contractors alike. With the airship images, Prince believed that U.S. military authorities would be able to see where those individuals retreated and could then track them down. Prince believed the airship was superior to anything the government had for such tasks, and he wanted to be the one to lease it out.

Prince didn't like to talk about how much money he was sinking into projects like the airship, yet his resources were ample. Besides his personal fortune, his company had seen an increase in revenue of some 600 percent in the past four years. In addition to research and development, the phenomenal growth would allow him to explore expansion opportunities in places like the Philippines, where Prince was toying with the idea of a jungle survival skills training center, a project Blackwater would later abandon after a groundswell of opposition. (Some Filipino lawmakers were concerned that the company might use the training center as recruiting grounds for third-country nationals to send to Iraq or Afghanistan.)

PRINCE WOULD FIND more success in Southern California, where Blackwater wanted to build a comprehensive center it could use to train sailors for the U.S. Navy. It made sense to locate the building in San Diego County, as the Navy had a massive base there. But this plan, too, like the Philippines deal, was hindered by significant resistance from local politicians and protestors that eventually led to the company's scrapping a development plan in Potrero, California, and delayed the center's opening at Otay Mesa, California, by weeks. The Blackwater reputation, it seemed, was already exacting a toll on the company's business.

Prince didn't let it get him down. If there was a physical sign of his determination to expand his company despite the growing criticisms, it became apparent in April 2006, when company executives threw a grand opening celebration for Blackwater's new, nearly 67,000-square-foot administrative office on the Moyock campus. Hundreds of clients, potential clients, friends, and family members were invited to see just how massive the company had become. "We wanted to demonstrate that we weren't in the lodge anymore, that we were growing," explained Chris Taylor.

Blackwater's new administration building was believed to be the largest in the entire county, a massive combination of stone, steel, and glass. It sat near a small manmade lake that Blackwater used for shipboard training for sailors and often for early morning swims by Blackwater executives. The huge doors leading to the lobby had .50 caliber machine gun barrels for handles. With some 300 rooms, there was plenty of space for continued expansion: a concrete sign of Prince's optimism in the business.

It was under a crisp April sky that guests began to funnel onto the property for the gala unveiling. Prince stood outside, almost at attention, to welcome them. He was clad in sunglasses, a polo shirt, and military-style pants and boots. This was not your run-of-the-mill executive event.

After lunch in the building's cafeteria, the hundreds of guests took a guided tour around the property on buses. There were demonstrations on shooting ranges, shows of skill at the driving track, and a chance for guests to see up close how a Blackwater-trained team might clear a hostage house. As the tour wrapped up, Prince addressed the crowd under a tent on the front lawn of the administration building. He thanked them for coming and then publicly shared his vision for the company, telling the crowd what he had often told others only in private conversations.

"We're trying to do for the national security apparatus what FedEx did for the postal service," said Prince. "They did many of the same services better, faster, and cheaper."

FedEx had been born from a desire to redefine speed and reliability when it came to global shipping. The company famously challenged the postal service's monopoly on mail, through a loophole intended for courier services for special deliveries. Many believe FedEx's competition forced the postal service to become more efficient, offering its own priority-mail options faster and cheaper than before. The comparison appealed to Prince: the U.S. armed forces, he argued, should never become a complacent monopoly. But critics of privatization worried: if the government doesn't have a monopoly on the use of force, what does it have?

The crowd gathered outside the Blackwater headquarters was largely receptive to Prince's message. Critics weren't invited. Typical of the Blackwater stance with media, there were very few reporters invited either. Cofer Black also addressed the crowd, sharing his belief that Blackwater was meeting a need and would do it better than anyone else. When the executives were finished with their brief statements, the spectators were asked to step out from under the tent and turn their attention overhead. Almost perfectly on cue, an airplane appeared in the cloud-dotted sky. Out of it jumped members of Blackwater's new parachute team. The crowd watched as the men opened their chutes emblazoned with the Blackwater logo. They landed just steps from the building, directly on cue. This was the way Prince wanted the world to see his company.

THINGS LOOKED DIFFERENT from Washington. Congress and the media had growing lists of questions about Blackwater, and the use of private contractors in general, but they would learn that finding someone who had the answers was a frustrating, time-consuming task. One might assume that the man at the top of the administration that had overseen the dramatic explosion of the private military industry would have had a grasp on just how the American military machine was being propped up. But in April 2006, more than three years after the start of the Iraq War, President George Bush was very publicly naive about the growing contractor phenomenon. When the president spoke at Johns Hopkins University, a student asked him a question that she had already put to Defense Secretary Donald Rumsfeld, who had failed to offer a satisfactory answer: "What law governs contractors?"

> THE PRESIDENT: *I was going to ask him. Go ahead.*
> *(Laughter.) Help. (Laughter.)*
> Q: *I was hoping your answer might be a little more specific.*
> *(Laughter.) Mr. Rumsfeld answered that Iraq has its own*
> *domestic laws, which he assumed applied to those private*
> *military contractors. However, Iraq is clearly not cur-*
> *rently capable of enforcing its laws, much less against—*
> *over our American military contractors. I would submit*
> *to you that in this case, this is one case that privatization*
> *is not a solution. And, Mr. President, how do you pro-*
> *pose to bring private military contractors under a system*
> *of law?*
> THE PRESIDENT: *I appreciate that very much. I wasn't*
> *kidding—(Laughter.) I was going to—I pick up the phone*
> *and say, Mr. Secretary, I've got an interesting question.*
> *(Laughter.) This is what delegation—I don't mean to be*
> *dodging the question, although it's kind of convenient in*
> *this case, but never—(Laughter.) I really will—I'm going to*
> *call the Secretary and say you brought up a very valid ques-*
> *tion, and what are we doing about it? That's how I work.*
> *I'm—thanks. (Laughter.)*

The clip of President Bush stumbling on the question became a hit on YouTube and made it more than clear that answers wouldn't be coming from the White House.

In early June 2006, Congress formally went to the source for answers by inviting the three major contractors for the State Department to testify at a hearing of the House Government Reform Committee on National Security, Emerging Threats, and International Relations. The company executives were asked to talk about private security firms and their standards and cooperation on the battlefield. The hearing was chaired by Connecticut Republican Christopher Shays.

Executives from Blackwater, Triple Canopy, and DynCorp were asked to attend. The congressional committee also invited Doug Brooks, a former graduate student who had turned his own interest in the industry into a proindustry lobby-type group he named the International Peace Operations Association. It was a voluntary organization that would, in essence, try to get the industry to police itself. To join, members had to agree to abide by a set of standards and could be called before the group's ethics committee if their company violated them. Blackwater was actively involved in the organization: Blackwater vice president Chris Taylor served as its chairman.

Prince was scheduled to be traveling on the date of the hearing and wasn't inclined to change his plans to take a seat in the limelight. A flurry of discussions was launched as Blackwater executives debated who to send in his place. There were a number of people in the company who had experience testifying before Congress: Schmitz, Richer, and Black. They had all offered to go, but ultimately none of them were sent. Prince decided that Chris Taylor would testify, even though Taylor had never done anything like that before. It caused concern at headquarters.

But Prince had made up his mind, and there was little more to say. With the Republicans in the majority, Taylor was confident of friendly treatment, as most of the criticism Blackwater had received to date had come from the left. Taylor had long been pushing for the company to take a more prominent role in public, an argument that had often met with support from others in the senior Blackwater management, but all such discussion usually ended the same way, with a reminder that regardless of what they thought they *should* do to get their message out, the State Department had bound them by contract to stay quiet. Taylor was looking forward to his testimony, a chance to publicly get his company's message out there.

Accompanying Taylor in the hearing room on June 13 were Gary Jackson, Blackwater attorney Steve Capace, and Paul Behrends. The four men filed into the crowded hearing room and took their seats, even though Taylor would not be testifying until a later session. Taylor wanted to hear what the first panel of the day had to say. Early on, some of the Democratic members of the committee started throwing out some pretty tough questions on issues like Fallujah. Taylor started sending e-mails back to Moyock in anticipation that he might be asked similar questions. He hadn't worked on that contract, but he wanted to be prepared for whatever might be coming his way.

Finally, Taylor's panel was up. In his opening statement, he laid out one of Prince's favorite arguments in support of using private military contractors:

> *Since the American Revolution, private security firms have played an integral role in the successful development and defense of our nation. The role of the private security firm has not changed that much over time. Providing specialized*

capabilities and surge capacity to the U.S. government in flex-
ible, cost-effective packages, and building capacity for friendly
foreign governments continue to be core competencies of our
industry.

His testimony shed light not only on what Blackwater was
doing for the U.S. government, but also on what it wanted to do.

Today, private security firms perform a number of roles from
executive protection and static security, to training partner na-
tions, to providing both ground and aviation logistics support,
all in dangerous environments. In the future private security
firms will likely be called upon to support stability operations
and peacekeeping efforts.

But the idea of Blackwater as peacekeepers couldn't be further from reality in the minds of some of the committee members. They were more concerned with the controversial issue of
accountability, and whether it even existed in the private military
industry. Taylor was ready for the question. He had armed himself with a list of applicable laws.

Our services support primarily federal entities. Private secu-
rity firms, therefore, are accountable to many domestic federal
statutes, regulations, and common law, which include the
Military Extraterritorial Jurisdiction Act, the War Crimes
Act of 1996, the Victims of Trafficking and Violence Protec-
tion Act of 2000, the Anti-Torture Statute, the Defense Trade
Controls Act, the Gun Control Act, Arms Export Control
Act, Export Administration Regulations, International Traffic
and Arms Regulations, the Defense Base Act, Federal Aviation

Regulations, the Defense Federal Acquisition Regulations, the
Foreign Corrupt Practices Act, and the general order of Cen-
tral Command, the Multinational Corps of Iraqi Forces, and
the Combined Joint Task Force 76.

The list sounded impressive. There was just one problem: not
a single private military contractor had been held accountable
under any of those laws. What good was a law if it wasn't ever
enforced?

Taylor's co-panelists took turns fielding general questions
about the industry. Sitting on the panel with Taylor was General
Robert Rosenkranz, a retired Army major general who went to
work for DynCorp International. Rosenkranz was also the president of DynCorp International's Technical Services Division.
His company had provided law enforcement services, coun-
ternarcotic support, logistical support, infrastructure development, and security services in places like Iraq and Afghanistan.
The other company sharing the State Department's Worldwide
Personal Protective Services contract, Triple Canopy, was rep-
resented by Ignacio Balderas, the company's chief executive officer. Triple Canopy was founded in 2003 by a group of U.S. Army
Special Forces veterans. Like the others, the company provided
"personal security details, fixed-site security, threat assessments,
and counterterrorism training." Triple Canopy had employees
working in Africa, Asia, the Middle East, and the United States.
While all of the companies present at the hearing provided similar services, they had very different experiences with the media—
and very different approaches to handling negative headlines.

Some of the Democrats on the committee focused on Taylor.
Congressman Dennis Kucinich of Ohio led the charge as he
zeroed in on some of the more notorious Blackwater stories that

had made headlines. Kucinich's questions ran the gamut from the bridge in Fallujah to how much money the company was being paid by the U.S. government. Taylor didn't have the answers to many of his questions. The funding in particular tripped Taylor up. Kucinich was insistent on finding out just how much money the private company was making from the U.S. government.

"And in those contracts, is it true that you were paying your men $600 a day but billing Regency [a Kuwait-based hotel chain] $815 a day?" asked Representative Kucinich.

"Per the presentation, Mr. Kucinich, $815 a day is the right figure, but it's a fully burdened figure. That includes travel, training, gear, housing, food—the works," answered Taylor.

Maryland Democrat Chris Van Hollen, in his turn, cited an article in the *Raleigh News & Observer* that said Blackwater had billed separately for overhead costs, above and beyond the $215 difference between the bill and what the men on the ground were being paid.

"That article," the congressman began,

and this is an opportunity to correct the article if you want—it said that the Blackwater charges to [Regency] for [Jerry] Zovko's work—he was one of the individual contractors involved in that terrible incident—were $815 a day—a markup of $215. It then goes on to say, "In addition, Blackwater billed the Regency separately for all its overhead and costs in Iraq— insurance, room and board, travel, weapons, ammunition, vehicle, office space." In other words, they said that you billed separately for that overhead, and you're saying—I just want to make it clear—you're saying that that overhead was part of the $815-a-day charge?

Taylor continued to insist that the $815 figure included over-head, and the committee came down hard on him for it.

"Well, they never used the word *lied,* but they said it appears it wasn't true," Taylor later recounted. "There is a legal account-ing definition of fully burdened that they were using, and I was using it more as a business vernacular."

As the Blackwater team walked out of the hearing, Gary Jack-son turned to Taylor and said, "You earned your salary today."

IF MEMBERS OF CONGRESS were looking for accountability for private contractors, they began to see signs of it in August 2006. David Passaro, a contractor for the Central Intelligence Agency, was found guilty of assaulting a detainee he interrogated at a military base in Afghanistan three years earlier. He was the first civilian contractor convicted of any wrongdoing in the twenty-first century. Though he didn't work for Blackwater, his case was a harbinger of trouble for the industry. The detainee Passaro had questioned later died of his injuries. Passaro wasn't convicted for the death, because there was no direct evidence that beating the man—with a flashlight—caused his death. Instead, Passaro was convicted of assault in connection with the death, news that didn't sit well with CIA Director Michael Hayden.

Hayden had taken the helm at the spy agency just months earlier. With a background in the Air Force and experience in just about every government intelligence agency you can think of—and some you probably can't—Hayden had worked with contractors before, and he wasn't going to let the news of Passa-ro's conviction cast a shadow over the CIA.

Hayden issued a statement after news of the conviction broke, saying, "I think it is very important for all of us to bear in mind that Passaro's actions were unlawful, reprehensible, and neither authorized nor condoned by the Agency." He went on to outline the investigative steps that had been followed after the allegations first came to light in 2003. "They were reported to managers in the field and relayed to headquarters. The CIA's Inspector General immediately began an investigation and referred the matter to the Department of Justice for criminal prosecution."

Hayden emphasized the point one more time, for good measure: "As abhorrent as this situation was, it is a fact that we, as an Agency, did not sweep it under a rug. We addressed it head-on and dealt with it swiftly."

Just months later, the State Department would grapple with a serious allegation of wrongdoing made against one of its contractors. This time it was a Blackwater man, and it would be handled *much* differently.

ANDREW MOONEN was working under Blackwater's State Department contract as a firearms technician in Baghdad in 2006. He was one of several contractors who attended a Christmas Eve celebration inside the Green Zone, a celebration that included alcohol. Moonen had been drinking—some say heavily—by 11:00 p.m. when he decided to leave the party. He was armed with a 9 mm Glock. The circumstances surrounding what happened next are a matter of dispute, but the one certainty is that Moonen shot and killed an Iraqi man, a guard for Iraq's vice president.

Moonen's lawyer says that his client got lost in the Green Zone after leaving the party and that Moonen was confronted by the guard as he neared the compound of Iraqi prime minister Nuri al-Maliki. Moonen's version of events is that the guard either pointed or fired his weapon at him. "Afraid for his life," said his lawyer, "Moonen fired his pistol, hitting the Iraqi three times."

Moonen ran to a nearby guard post manned by contractors from Triple Canopy. There were no known witnesses to the shooting itself.

The following hours would see a flurry of messages back and forth between Baghdad, Moyock, and the State Department. Moonen told investigators on Christmas Day that he had fired the shots in self-defense after the bodyguard shot at him. Blackwater fired him nonetheless for possessing a firearm while under the influence of alcohol. The next day, at the direction of the State Department, Blackwater transported Moonen to Jordan and then flew him back to the United States. Blackwater and the State Department kept the incident quiet and tried to figure out how to handle the outraged Iraqi government. The State Department suggested that money be paid to the man's family and forwarded figures ranging from $15,000 to $250,000 to Blackwater management.

The House Government and Oversight Committee would later bring the incident to the public's attention by releasing a report that detailed e-mails back and forth in the case, including one by an embassy security official that read, "This was an unfortunate event, but we feel that it doesn't reflect on the overall Blackwater performance. They do an exceptional job under very challenging circumstances. We would like to help them resolve this so we can continue with our protective mission."

The decision to keep things quiet was made by the State Department, yet within months, the incident would become public, directing outrage and suspicion toward Blackwater. Prince was frustrated with the situation. His company was doing what it was told by the client. The contract with the U.S. State Department forbade him from talking to the media about anything without prior permission. But Blackwater wasn't a branch of the government; it was a private business, and it was taking a beating by staying silent.

Prince would later testify to a congressional committee that his company did all it could in the aftermath of the shooting by firing and fining Moonen thousands of dollars. "We as a private company cannot detain him. We can fire, we can fine, but we can't do anything else," Prince testified.

But the decision to keep the incident quiet would have other repercussions. Within two months, Andrew Moonen would be back at work with a Defense Department contractor in Kuwait. The decision of what to do with Moonen would remain unanswered for more than a year as U.S. authorities grappled with how to handle the case, and whether they even had jurisdiction to charge Moonen with any kind of crime. The Justice Department would work with U.S. attorneys to try to figure out whether they would, or could, charge and prosecute him. Almost a year and a half later, a team that included two federal prosecutors and an FBI agent would travel to Iraq seeking evidence.

WHILE 2006 WOULD END on a controversial note, 2007 would begin with another tragedy, this one bringing a significant loss of life at Blackwater.

On the morning of January 23, Prince was awakened by the grinding noise of his BlackBerry. It was an urgent e-mail from Gary Jackson. A Blackwater gunner working in Iraq had been shot in the head, life condition unknown. It was a brief note followed minutes later by another. They'd lost the gunner, and one helicopter was unaccounted for.

As Blackwater's aviation manager in Baghdad, Dan Laguna was the man responsible for tracking the travel routes of diplomatic convoys, routes that changed daily in an effort to keep insurgents from becoming familiar with diplomatic routines. If any of the ground teams got into trouble, Dan was the man who would launch air support.

It had been a quiet morning for Laguna when suddenly the radio crackled: "Team in contact, team in contact." The stress in the voice was unmistakable. Laguna listened carefully for clues about the details he needed: the team's location and what kind of trouble they were facing. Just then, the phone rang.

It was an urgent request from the tactical operations center (TOC). A ground team escorting U.S. diplomats in a volatile Baghdad neighborhood was under heavy insurgent fire. They needed help immediately.

Laguna's thirty years of military experience made situations like these seem almost normal, though the adrenaline still surged. A Green Beret before going to flight school, Dan knew from his time in the elite Special Operations unit Task Force 160 that time makes the critical difference between a rescue mission and a recovery mission. Laguna gave the order to get the helicopters in the air. From Landing Zone Washington, it would take them just minutes to reach the trouble.

From a helicopter, automatic fire can sound like a series of pops, or it can sound like nothing at all. The noise of the blades can drown out a small arms attack. As the two teams left the Green Zone, they began taking on automatic fire. A gunner was hit; his body fell from the chopper, still attached by the tether, dangling in midair.

"We've got a man down!" the pilot yelled into the radio, immediately scanning his surroundings for a place large enough to touch down. They needed to get the body back in the aircraft as soon as possible. A rooftop a few streets away was the only refuge.

It took the men just minutes to pull the gunner's body back into the chopper. They had to get him back to the Green Zone hospital. The pilot lifted off again, turning the chopper in a furious circle of dust. "We're heading back," he signaled to the other pilot. "We're coming with you," was the response. Little birds never fly alone in Baghdad.

Laguna was still monitoring every move on the radio. When he heard that his men were leaving the scene to head to the hospital, he knew he had to get another team out there to provide cover for the ground crew, still under attack. He was already on it, when another desperate phone call came in from the embattled team.

Dan ordered his men to ready his own chopper. Dozens of guys had heard the news by now, many of them offering to help, but Dan asked the one man he knew and trusted to be his wingman in a second chopper—his brother, Arthur. Arthur had spent thirty-four years in the military and was a full-time pilot with the National Guard before Dan convinced him to retire and come to work for Blackwater. It took their two choppers about three minutes to get to the location. Almost immediately, they began taking on rounds of automatic fire. It seemed like it was coming from everywhere.

It was "the most volume of fire that I have ever seen in my career," Dan recalled, "heavy volumes of light automatic fire and heavy weapon fire."

They started taking evasive measures. Dan turned his bird to the south and could see his brother's aircraft out of the corner of his eye. Suddenly, he heard his brother's voice on the radio: "We're taking rounds! I'm hit, I'm hit! We're going back."

By the time he turned around to get a better look at the damage to his brother's chopper, the sky was empty. Arthur Laguna and his crew were nowhere to be seen.

Dan searched the skyline for smoke, signs of a crash, but saw nothing but the clear blue sky. He began flying along the narrow alleyways looking for his brother's chopper, trying hard to ignore the fire his own aircraft was taking on. He called to request a search and rescue team. He wasn't going to leave until he found his brother and his crew.

Dan couldn't hear the bullets as they hit his chopper, but it was evident that the little bird had been hit several times. Finally, his team made a plea: land right away, or they might not make it. Dan scanned the horizon for a semisafe spot and found it a few streets away in a courtyard. Dan and one of the pilots took a look at the damage, noticing the holes in the fuselage first. When the blades slowed enough to get a good look, he saw a hole in one of them, big enough to stick a foot through. He also noticed a crowd of men off to the east, running toward them. They'd seen the helicopter come down. Dan and his men jumped back into the chopper, thankful that the little bird still had enough power to limp back to the landing zone.

A quick blade change and they were back in the air, back near the spot where Arthur had vanished. U.S. Army troops had already arrived and were engaged in a heated battle with insurgents. Dan's chopper began circling, providing air cover and searching for signs of the downed chopper.

Dan called for his brother over the radio every five seconds. "Art, Art, Art, where are you at?"

Finally, Dan spotted the wreckage in a small alley. It was just minutes before he saw the body bags. There was heavy gunfire all around.

With no safe place to land, Dan, in desperation, landed the bird right in the middle of the street, in the middle of the firefight.

"I'm jumping out; you guys go back to the Green Zone, I'll find my way back when I can."

"No, we're staying with you, boss; we're staying right here."

As he stepped out of the helicopter, an RPG, or rocket-propelled grenade, went off over his head. There was smoke everywhere.

He made his way a hundred feet or so, in the middle of the raging battle, to the body bags. He knelt by the first one, oblivious to the bullets flying around him.

He began unzipping the bags one by one. Arthur was in the second bag.

Dan heard a voice coming from behind a Stryker vehicle: "Get the hell out of there!"

It was an Army major.

"I want you to promise me that these guys will be brought back to the Green Zone," Dan yelled.

"We'll do it; now, get out," returned the major.

Arthur's death and the deaths of his colleagues, Casey Casavant, Steve Gernet, Ronald Johnson, and Shane Stanfield, would not be recorded by the Pentagon. The U.S. military doesn't count contractors who are killed in battle, though with more than a thousand private military contractors killed in Iraq, taking their deaths into consideration more accurately reflects the total human cost of the war.

Arthur's widow, Marybeth Laguna, understood the cost of the war. At her husband's funeral just days after his death, she was surprised at the outpouring of support. Some two thousand people attended. Traffic was blocked on a heavily traveled stretch of Sacramento road for nearly an hour. "It was shocking," said

Marybeth Laguna. "He was so humble." But word had spread that a former member of law enforcement in California had fallen. Police officers from small communities miles away made the trip to show their respect. Both Blackwater and the State Department sent representatives. To Marybeth, the Blackwater guards were heroes; she saw it no other way. Several months later she would work with the company to submit an editorial that was published in the *Washington Post,* calling her husband a Blackwater hero and insisting that he lived his life in service to his country, whether it was as a member of the military or as a private contractor. She admitted that Blackwater's spokeswoman actually wrote much of the letter, but she insisted that it was exactly what she wanted to say.

JUST DAYS AFTER Laguna and his colleagues' deaths, another Blackwater executive would be in the congressional hot seat, and this time the Democrats controlled the gavel. They had won control of Congress in the November 2006 election. Among the first orders of business for Henry Waxman, the new Democratic chair of the House Committee on Oversight and Government Reform, was to get answers to some of the questions about military contractors that had not been aggressively pursued when the Republicans controlled Congress. Prince was invited, but he sent general counsel Andrew Howell in his place. Also invited were family members of the Fallujah victims.

Katy Helvenston had been looking forward to this day for a long time. While she had spoken out in several newspaper articles and had made TV news appearances about her quest to get more answers out of Blackwater, she hadn't testified before a congressional committee before. The testimony soon became emotional, as family members recalled how their loved ones had been shot and beaten, with some of them set on fire and dragged through the streets. The families blamed Blackwater for sending the men into the situation unprepared. Blackwater executives, including Prince, viewed the hearing as little more than a political strike against the company. Howell didn't mince words, calling the hearing an "obvious attempt by the plaintiffs' lawyers to use this hearing for their own purposes." He was supported by Republican Congressman Tom Davis, who said, "This is not the forum to prosecute private lawsuits, or the place to exploit a tragic event for political purposes."

Waxman shot back, telling Davis the hearing was about "four men who lost their lives. I don't know whether they were Democrats or Republicans." The Democrats, led largely by Congressman Waxman and Congresswoman Jan Schakowsky of Illinois, were determined to get more answers about the use of private contractors, and just how much the Bush administration had come to rely on them.

Less than a month earlier, President Bush had gone on national television to announce a new "surge" of deployments to Iraq. He promised to increase the size of the active Army and Marine Corps, saying the increase was needed because "there were not enough Iraqi and American troops to secure neighborhoods that had been cleared of terrorists and insurgents."

Many saw the announcement as a public acknowledgment that the administration had made serious mistakes in estimating the numbers of troops it would take to do the job in Iraq. Many inside the Pentagon also saw it as a vindication of General Eric Shinseki. The former Army chief of staff had been marginalized by Rumsfeld for telling Congress just before the war began that the United States needed more troops to be successful in Iraq. The warning went unheeded. Shinseki retired in June 2003, still cautioning that the United States shouldn't try to carry out a "twelve-division strategy" with a "ten-division army."

Even if Rumsfeld had agreed with Shinseki at the time, the Pentagon simply didn't have the bodies to send to Iraq. That was the reason why Blackwater had earned its lucrative contract from the State Department to begin with. But when the Pentagon made the decision to have the State Department hire its own security, it didn't foresee that working with non-Pentagon-employed contractors would make for such a messy battlefield amid the civilian population in Iraq.

Members of the military working alongside the hired help would find poor coordination between the commanders on the battlefield and the contractors in Iraq, and it would become apparent in increasingly frustrating ways for leaders on the ground. Not only was it hard to know where the contractors were going, it was also hard to know where they had been. Contractors didn't drive around in marked vehicles, so telling one from the other was nearly impossible without stopping the convoys and questioning the people in them. Military leaders complained that contractor-protected convoys would blow through intersections, or even Iraqi police checkpoints, without bothering to stop. In one sign of stunningly aggressive behavior, an unidentified contractor ran a U.S. military Humvee off the road. Inside the Humvee was a very angry U.S. general.

According to a senior DoD official, the contractors in general, and Blackwater specifically, "were very difficult to work with, overly aggressive. Part of counterinsurgency is kicking down doors and getting people, but part of it is winning the people . . . how do you do that when they see Suburbans, with the guys with big muscles and machine guns hanging out the side, driving through checkpoints? There was a discipline problem."

IN MAY 2007, Prince decided to pen a letter to the *Grand Rapids Press* in response to an article the paper had printed about his company. He was upset that Blackwater was being dubbed a "mercenary army" by journalists he thought were left-leaning. Prince told the paper there was "nothing mercenary about Black-water activities," insisting that his contractors were professionals and patriots.

"Clearly," he wrote, "the mercenary label is intended to polar-ize the discussion and craft the most negative image possible of Blackwater. The highest authority on rhetoric, the Oxford Eng-lish Dictionary, however, defines 'mercenary' as 'a professional soldier serving a foreign power.' Blackwater does not now, nor has it ever, provided security services for, or on behalf of, any country other than the United States of America."

The devil, of course, is in the details. While Blackwater was in fact American owned, it had hired non-Americans to do its work in countries other than the United States. It also worked for other countries. But the technicality was that it had done both under the Greystone umbrella. While the companies were separate on paper, they were tied at the hip. Blackwater focused on U.S. government contracts, and Greystone focused on at-tracting both foreign governments and foreign businesses as cli-ents. The company wasn't as big as Blackwater, with just over two hundred employees, but it provided very similar services to foreign clients. Amman was the staging ground for third-country nationals moving in and out of Iraq. Greystone also worked with

a local company in the United Arab Emirates to provide training for UAE helicopter pilots and special operations troops. In
Iraq, the company provided security details for groups like the
International Republican Institute, which develops political parties and civic institutions and encourages youth-based advocacy
groups. Both John McCain and Paul Bremer served on the IRI's
board of directors.

IN MAY 2007 a Blackwater contractor shot and killed an Iraqi
driver near the Interior Ministry. Sadly, shootings of Iraqi drivers
were by now not uncommon. Several contractors working in the
country had opened fire into vehicles that they felt might pose a
threat. The very same week, in a separate incident, a Blackwater
convoy was ambushed in Baghdad, leading to a flurry of gunfire by Blackwater contractors who called for help from U.S. and
Iraqi troops. Blackwater declined to offer details on the incidents
publicly, but the shooting, reported to have lasted more than an
hour, angered many inside Iraq's Interior Ministry.

Iraqi Interior spokesman Major General Abdul-Karim Khalaf
would later add that Blackwater was being investigated by Iraqi authorities for two separate, earlier shootings, including one on February 7 when three guards at Iraqi State Television were killed.

Many in the Iraqi government saw the company's tactics as
overly aggressive. Some inside the Pentagon and in the U.S. Congress would come to share that opinion.

Was it possible that Blackwater had some out-of-control employees? Were the company's control structures anywhere near
as thorough as they should have been? Around the same time,
another explosive story was circulating. Federal investigators
wanted to know if the company had illegally smuggled weapons

into Iraq. The company denied it, and investigators remained tight-lipped. But tales that were emerging from former employees suggested that the Blackwater management had been in such a rush to get weapons into Iraq with as little bureaucracy as possible that it had shipped the weapons in large pallets with dog food. Since dog food is considered unsanitary in the Arab culture, there was little risk the arms would be detected. Blackwater denied smuggling in any form and shot back at what it called inaccurate media reports, insisting that the company had never shipped an automatic weapon into Iraq. Blackwater also insisted that it had obtained export licenses for the weapons it did ship, and that it never packed any weapons inside actual bags of dog food, as some reports claimed.

"The company has, however, packed shipping pallets with valuable and pilferable items, including weapons, interior to bags of dog food or other low-theft items. This common practice is done to prevent corrupt foreign customs agents and shipping workers from stealing the valuables. U.S. export statutes require licensing of controlled materials but do not dictate their placement within packaging," read the statement.

Blackwater acknowledged that it hadn't done everything right when it came to abiding by export laws. After a lengthy federal investigation, the company would announce the creation of an outside committee and the position of vice president of export compliance to help make sure it followed regulations more closely in the future. Federal investigators wouldn't elaborate on the details of their investigation.

Just two years earlier, Blackwater fired two employees, saying the men were stealing from the company. Blackwater reached out to the Bureau of Alcohol, Tobacco and Firearms to investigate. The two fired employees later pled guilty to possession of stolen firearms and agreed to cooperate with prosecutors in what was believed to be the expanded investigation.

With at least one part of the government investigating the company, and with the size of its contracts skyrocketing, Blackwater was in no position to alienate any more of its friends in Washington. Some Blackwater contacts at the State Department were already turning against the company, for its perceived cowboy attitude and bad public relations. Six months earlier, Chris Taylor had given an interview to the *Weekly Standard* that set teeth on edge at Foggy Bottom, and in May 2007, he left the company.

The article quoted Taylor talking about the moral importance the company placed on its work, saying Prince "believes to his core that this is his life's work. If you're not willing to drink the Blackwater Kool-aid and be committed to supporting humane democracy around the world, then there's probably a better place" for you. "Cofer [Black] and I have been speaking about our ability to help in Darfur ad infinitum, and that just pisses off the humanitarian world. They have problems with private security companies, not because of performance but because they think that in some cases it removes their ability to cross borders, to talk to both sides, to be neutral. And that's great, but the age-old question [is]—is neutrality greater than saving one more life? What's the marginal utility on one more life?" Taylor asked the reporter.

Some inside the State Department were furious. They considered the comments far too glib and were angry that the company hadn't first sought permission for the interview, as was required by their contract. On December 11, 2006, a senior contracting officer from the State Department fired off an angry e-mail to Blackwater executives handling the State Department contract, warning that the company had crossed the line.

> *Please see below parts of an article (some highlighted in blue) printed in the Weekly Standard and my comments (in red). I just don't know why Blackwater continually wants to draw attention to themselves and basically say, "Come and get me" to any investigating Congressional Committee. I've had it with the egos, the macho attitude and the total disregard of just how much trouble this will cause. Doesn't Chris Taylor understand that after January, there will be much more consentration [sic] on federal contracts—especially those in Iraq, Afghanistan and those that have been awarded under the Urgent/Compelling standards. For heaven's sake, someone get a handle on him. As for Mr. Prince, now the top man has insulted federal contracting officers and basically stated that Blackwater procurement personnel know so much more than the government contracting officers. I really needed this tid bit [sic] of information.*

The e-mail then reprints, with State Department comments in parentheses, much of the *Weekly Standard* article:

> *And there's much, much more. Sitting in his second-story office with expansive views of the grounds, Blackwater vice president for strategic initiatives and former recon Marine Chris Taylor makes a sound business case for the Blackwater facility. "One of the single greatest factors that makes us who we are today is, one, we are always complete, correct, and on time with our services and, two, this facility—this is*

*the greatest barrier to entry in the market of doing train-
ing and security operations; nobody else has this." Taylor
continues: "To build this facility today—$40 or $50 million, and nobody's got that kind of coin. Nobody wants to
invest that, especially if you are going into a market where
there already is a big dog." (Do you really think that other
companies will ignore this and not notify their representatives? "Look Mr. Representative, Blackwater is the big dog
and agencies are giving them all of the contracts." Hearings
to be scheduled.)*

*Blackwater is now one of the largest and most respected
suppliers of "private military contractors" (What did I tell
Blackwater about advertising themselves as a military/quasi-
military organization!) in Iraq. . . .*

*Aside from providing one of the most demoralizing images
of the war, the killing of the four Blackwater employees did
two major things. It was the catalyst for the Battle of Falluja,
a brutal but ultimately successful attempt to reclaim the city
from insurgents, which resulted in 83 additional U.S. troops
killed in action. And it drew national attention to the use of
private contractors—"mercenaries" to their more vehement
detractors—in Iraq. (Do you really want the families of dead
service personnel to read that their son/daughter died because
four Blackwater employees got killed?)*

*Blackwater objects to the use of the m-word for its
employees, preferring the term "private military contractors." (Why did I waste my time telling Blackwater why this
definition could not be used?) For one thing, "mercenary"
is not accurate. Private military contractors in Iraq do not
execute offensive operations—they only provide security,
and their rules of engagement are to use proportionate force*

only when attacked. (It is too late to define the words after the
image is presented—military is military is military.) . . .

In fact, Blackwater objects to its personnel being tarred
as mercenaries mainly because they regard it as an assault on
their character and their professionalism. (How about saying
you don't like it because you are not mercenaries—no, let's get
macho again and say that the term is insulting.) "We're in nine
different countries," says Chris Taylor, "probably have about
2,300 people deployed today, another 21,000 in our database,
and these are people the majority of whom have already had
a career in public service, either military or law enforcement,
who are honorably discharged, who have any number of medals
for heroism. Yet we still have to face
critics who say everybody is a mercenary—they're only out for a
buck."

. . . Blackwater CEO Erik Prince, the company's founder,
"believes to his core that this is his life's work," says Taylor.
"If you're not willing to drink the Blackwater Kool-aid and
be committed to supporting humane democracy around the
world, then there's probably a better place" to go work, "be-
cause that's all we do." (Do you have any idea the image this
brings up? "Blackwater Kool-aid": what in the #$%^ are you
thinking.)

Of all of the charges leveled at Blackwater, one of the most
damning is that they are war profiteers. And it's a charge the
company is eager to defend against, especially in light of the
fact that it has been awarded numerous CIA and other no-bid
"urgent and compelling need" contracts by the government,
the terms of which are often shrouded in secrecy. (Here we go
again, get the files ready to take to the hill. More work caused
by a big mouth.)

"One of the best ways the U.S. government overall, particularly the DoD, can get better value for the taxpayers is by improving the training, standards, and competence of their own contracting officers," he says. "When you go to sell to a Fortune 500 company, their purchasing officer knows more about your process than you do—they really drill down; they know the best value and they expect execution complete, correct, and on time. With government contracting officers that's not always the case; that's seldom the case. There's a lot more shortcomings that are allowed that go unpunished." (Thanks for the hit on my career field. I will remember that this is Blackwater's institutional opinion. This tells me that I need to begin formal audits in order to protect the taxpayer, because after all, as a federal contracting officer, I just can't match up to the brilliant corporate purchasing officers from Blackwater.)

. . . Black water [sic] has earned $505 million in publicly identifiable contracts since 2000—it's no wonder private military contractors jokingly refer to themselves as the "Coalition of the Billing." (Again, thanks for the education.)

As for the individual contractors on the ground, pay varies, but $600–$700 a day would not be out of line for a qualified armed guard, and higher figures are commonplace, depending on qualifications and experience. The good pay is a bit of a joke within the industry. Circulating on the message boards and e-mail lists of contractors for some time has been this tongue-in-cheek but nonetheless revealing "Contractor's Creed": I care not for ribbons and awards for valor. I do this job for the opportunity to kill the enemies of my country, and to finally get that boat I've always wanted. In any combat zone, I will always locate the swimming pool, beer, and women, because I can. I will deploy on my terms, and if it ever gets too stupid, I will simply find another company that pays me more. *(I hope Blackwater can stand being painted with this brush.)*

Despite the ethical perils inherent in such work, Prince insists not just that the future of warfare depends on private companies driving market efficiencies, but that this is the way of the world. "I would go back to a deeper view of history. The idea of private contractors doing this kind of work is not a recent phenomenon," he says. He can rattle off any number of examples of mercenaries being used throughout history—many of whom were beloved figures in U.S. history, from Revolutionary hero Lafayette to the Flying Tigers in World War II. (All offensive driven comparisons. You're really batting 1.000.)

Blackwater thinks it has the answer. "I just got back from Darfur," says Chris Taylor, the vice president for strategic initiatives. "I called Erik on my sat phone and said, 'I was in Juba; there's 300 U.N. vehicles in a motor pool, there's any number of NGOs driving within a one-mile radius within Juba, and nothing's getting done. The only time you see people in their vehicles is when they were going to the tent cities, because there's a bar in every tent city." (Chris, you just had to go there didn't you? Next, you'll bring Cofer Black into the mix.)

Blackwater vice-chairman Cofer Black, a former CIA agent and State Department coordinator for counterterrorism, made waves at a conference in Amman, Jordan, earlier this year saying the company is ready to provide brigade-size forces (1,500–3,000 soldiers) for peacekeeping missions around the world. Reflecting on his experience in Darfur,

Taylor says the solution to the situation is obvious. "I'm not
really good at math but it seems like a pretty simple equa-
tion to solve. Get more people, skilled people, in there. Even
in Darfur today, [there are only] 7,000 African Union troops
in a place the size of France," Taylor says. "So why not send
us?" (See above. Macho, "Look at Me" attitude. I warned
you, but you just don't listen.)

Blackwater insists it is different. Prince and Black water
[sic] have been involved in charities on the margins of the
humanitarian world for some time now. But the resistance
is fierce. "Cofer and I have been speaking about our abil-
ity to help in Darfur ad infinitum, and that just pisses off
the humanitarian world," Taylor says. "They have problems
with private security companies, not because of performance
but because they think that in some cases it removes their
ability to cross borders, to talk to both sides, to be neutral.
And that's great, but the age-old question [is]—is neutrality
greater than saving one more life? What's the marginal util-
ity on one more life?" (Your ego is going to create a massive
amount of work for government personnel. You know what
is going to happen now—hearings and testimony on the
hill. Chris, I hope you are quite satisfied. I told you to keep
quiet.)

Besides the State Department employee's perspective laid out
in the e-mail, Blackwater made one crucial mistake: it failed to
run the request to grant the interviews to the *Weekly Standard*
past its contracting officer at the State Department.

James "Steve" Rogers was the man in charge of overseeing
Blackwater's contract with the State Department. He was also
a former Air Force man from the Vietnam era, and he defined

"no-nonsense." After the article appeared, he summoned Prince to his office. He knew about the company's problems with the media and how the department had been thrown into damage control after Cofer Black's comments about being ready to play on someone's team in Amman, Jordan, just months earlier.

Prince came to the meeting prepared to defend the contract, but instead he faced a serious warning about Jackson and Taylor. "Keep them quiet, or you're off the contract," Rogers said, according to one of the parties present at the meeting. "Stop the macho stance of not running stuff through me first."

But there were also those inside State who criticized the government itself for some of Blackwater's problems. One State Department employee, who remains anonymous because he didn't have permission to speak to the media, said that the government got it wrong more often than Blackwater did. When it came to Blackwater's moving weapons into Iraq, the employee said, "We paid the contractor because *we* couldn't get the weapons over there. The federal government couldn't get off their butt and get them; they were bogged down in damned bureaucracy. It was so much easier to contract it out."

And he couldn't deny the power Prince was garnering among some in government offices. "The guy is huge; he's big, he's visible. What are you gonna do? He can buy and sell you."

Financially, Blackwater had a lot riding on making the State Department happy; it was bidding for yet another lucrative contract, this one for helicopters in Iraq. Largely because of the fallout from the *Weekly Standard* article, the decision was made that Taylor had to go. Jackson made the announcement at one of the company's 7:45 a.m. meetings for executives. Taylor was leaving Blackwater and taking a position with Greystone in Amman. Jackson characterized the move in no uncertain terms, saying that Taylor was taking a "shotgun blast to the face for all of us." Taylor eventually left Greystone as well and enrolled in a master's degree program at Harvard before taking a high-level position with another defense contractor. But the message was clear: when it came to making the State Department happy, the company had its limits. While Prince hadn't sought permission to grant interviews and access for the cover story in the first place, once the customer got angry enough, steps were taken to appease it.

CHAPTER 8

September 16, 2007

"Something terrible happened in Nisoor Square, and somebody,
someday will figure out what happened, maybe."

–AMBASSADOR PATRICK KENNEDY

A MAN RAISED with a focus on family, Erik Prince spent most Sundays with his wife and kids. Sunday, September 16, was no different. But even on a weekend, Prince kept the BlackBerry close; he had too many balls in the air to be away from it for long. Sometime in the afternoon, Prince got an e-mail warning him that the *Washington Post* was working on a story about a shooting incident in Baghdad that involved his men. That was how Prince first heard about the event that would place his security company squarely in the center of the contractor debate, and bring the issue of private military contractors to the forefront of Washington's agenda at long last.

Prince called Danny Carroll, his site manager in Baghdad, to find out what had happened: "He said, 'Boss, the guys were locked in position, holding the traffic circle, and they got fired on, and they shot back.'" The question, though, was who fired first? And how much firepower did the Blackwater men unleash? It would take more than a year to piece it all together.

Investigators had little to go on initially, but there were a few things they knew for certain. A Blackwater team had escorted U.S. officials to a development meeting outside the Green Zone. Sometime before noon local time, a bomb exploded nearby. The decision was made to evacuate. As the diplomats piled into vehicles and headed back toward the Green Zone, another convoy moved ahead to clear the way. Their route took them through a busy neighborhood intersection known as Nisoor Square.

According to early reports, no fewer than four vehicles on the advance team stopped local traffic, and some Blackwater guards in that team got out of their SUVs. Within minutes at least one of the Blackwater guards began to fire. His bullets are believed to have struck and killed the driver of one nearby car. According to an initial investigation, the situation escalated quickly into a bloody, chaotic scene. When it was over, somewhere between fourteen and seventeen Iraqis would lie dead, some of them on the street, some in their cars in puddles of blood.

Not yet aware of the full extent of what had happened, Prince thought to himself it was going to be another long, crappy week. Gary Jackson felt the same. After all, a shooting in Baghdad was a common thing for the company, which routinely found itself under attack. "I thought another day in Baghdad," said Jackson. "We have them all the time."

In the days just prior to September 16, Blackwater personnel had been involved in two particularly dramatic incidents. One involved a helicopter that was shot at by insurgents. The attack was so severe that it blew the tail boom off the helicopter while it was still in the air. The pilot managed to land safely on the ground.

In the other incident, a heavily armored vehicle known as a Puma was hit with an EFP, an explosively formed projectile. It's a shape charge that, when detonated, melts into molten copper or glass that can pierce even heavy armor. "They're very dangerous, even in heavily armored vehicles, like Bradley fighting vehicles," said a Blackwater employee. "If they're difficult to defeat in a Bradley, you can imagine what they can do to a Puma, which is a commercially available vehicle." The attack on the Puma injured some of the Blackwater employees inside, one of them so seriously that he had to be airlifted to a medical facility for treatment.

BY THE TIME Prince woke up in McLean, Virginia, on the morning of Monday, September 17, media headlines were screaming that Iraq's Interior Ministry was accusing his men of nothing less than murder. The ministry was telling reporters that the Blackwater guards had opened fire unprovoked, perpetrating a savage massacre. There were varying counts of the dead, ranging from eleven to twenty. Prince was furious. He had been told by his men that the team in Nisoor Square was attacked by insurgents wearing Iraqi police uniforms, and that they were only responding in self-defense. He believed them. He had already seen the initial State Department account filed on the incident, known as the SPOT report. Written on Bureau of Diplomatic Security letterhead, the two-page report recorded Blackwater's same-day perspective on what had happened:

> TST 23 [the convoy] entered an intersection identified as Gray 87 when they were engaged with small arms fire. Estimated 8–10 persons fired from multiple nearby locations, with some aggressors dressed in civilian apparel and others in Iraqi Police uniforms. The team returned defensive fire and attempted to drive out [away from] the initial ambush site; however, the

team command Bearcat vehicle was disabled during the attack and could not continue.

While the SPOT report is intended to serve only as a first-blush account of an incident, it is still an official U.S. government report. Ironically, the creation of the report was a responsibility that had been assigned to contractors, working in the State Department's Regional Security Office in Baghdad. On this day, the person writing the SPOT report was a Blackwater contractor. The State Department would later play down the report, saying it had no standing whatsoever. What else could they say? The Pentagon already employed contractors to coordinate its contractors. Now, the State Department was employing Blackwater contractors who were in a position to report on other Blackwater contractors.

Prince and his top advisers didn't believe the Iraqi Interior Ministry's account of events. Rob Richer, among others, assumed that the details were being twisted for political purposes. "Our guys wouldn't overreact," Richer later maintained. "And you can't believe anything the Iraqis say."

But the Interior Ministry's account was spreading quickly via international news networks and blogs. Gary Jackson saw a spiraling PR problem. "The [Interior Ministry] makes a statement and then the American press picks up on it and then the bloggers pick up on it," recalled Jackson, who had spent a good part of his morning checking the headlines on various blogs and news Web sites. "I could see it spinning out of control, like a fire, a brush fire."

Prince was determined not to let his company become the victim of a falsehood. He was convinced this was nothing more than a politically charged attack. Early Monday morning he started calling the people he knew and trusted in the media. It was a short list. He was furious that the Interior Ministry's side of the story was being reported, he thought, without question.

The Blackwater version of what happened was not impossible to believe. September 2007 was a low point in Iraq, just before President Bush proposed a surge in troops. There had been other incidents of Iraqis and Americans coming under fire from insurgents dressed in Iraqi police uniforms. Just ten days before the shooting, retired Marine general James Jones presented *The Report of the Independent Commission on the Security Forces of Iraq,* a comprehensive look at the readiness of Iraqi Security Forces to assume responsibility for security in their own country. It examined their ability to deny international terrorists safe haven and to bring an end to sectarian violence. The report found that "[t]he Ministry of Interior is a ministry in name only" and that, "given the level of sectarian infiltration within the Ministry of Interior, as well as the decentralized nature of the Iraqi Police Service, the concerted efforts of ministry officials and Coalition advisors will be required not only to develop and implement a system that is able to accurately account for issued equipment but also to foster a culture of accountability within the MOI."

The Blackwater team in Nisoor Square was working under the direction of a regional security officer, referred to as the RSO on a good day and a myriad of not-so-flattering nicknames on others. The RSO worked for the State Department's Diplomatic Security Service and was, essentially, the State Department's person in charge on the ground. On September 16, there was no RSO in the advance team convoy, so the State Department had no eyewitness of its own. Still, Prince was absolutely adamant that his men had done nothing outside the realm of their contract. He was furious that the State Department was saying nothing in public in defense of them.

On Monday afternoon, Prince called Ambassador Richard Griffin at the Diplomatic Security Office in Virginia. He knew that he couldn't talk to the media without State Department permission, and he was determined to get it. "I said, 'Sir, if you don't say something to defend the company, I'm going to,'" recalled Prince. The answer back was to sit tight, that a response was being coordinated by State.

Days passed with no real coordinated response to the Interior Ministry's accusations. Anonymous sources started leaking information to American reporters that told a very different story from the one Prince believed. One source suggested that no evidence had been found at the scene to indicate that the Blackwater employees came under attack. Then, as now, Prince insisted he saw photographs of his vehicles with bullet holes. To make matters worse, Richer believed the anonymous sources saying the opposite were within the U.S. military.

"We were told that our people acted appropriately, and then we started seeing leaks coming out of the DoD," remembered Richer. "Erik was increasingly frustrated."

Richer believed that some people at the Pentagon didn't like the way Blackwater operated. They saw Prince and his men as arrogant, and they were looking for payback. Even those in the State Department had tied the company's hands, he thought, by not allowing them to go public with a statement to the media.

"We can't defend ourselves," said Richer, "and the client was saying don't talk to the press." Prince and his executives were forced to sit back and watch as the news about Blackwater turned from bad to worse. Some Iraqis had begun to offer staggering accounts of innocent people being gunned down as they tried to flee the hail of gunfire inflicted by the Blackwater guards. One witness told investigators that he heard a Blackwater guard yell,

"No, no, no" after the shooting began, indicating a difference of opinion among the contractors over the escalation of force.

The Iraqi government continued to call the incident nothing less than murder and demanded millions in compensation for the victims' families. But because of Blackwater's immunity from local laws, the Iraqi government actually had little legal recourse, even in its own country. This was a battle to be fought in the political arena. Iraqi officials demanded that the State Department fire the company.

THE SHOOTING sent the U.S. State Department into crisis mode. Iraq's government threatened to halt Blackwater's ability to operate in the country, something that would have severely crippled State Department personnel outside the heavily fortified Green Zone. Blackwater made up a huge part of the security team for its diplomats and reconstruction officials. Getting safely from point A to point B was critical to the mission. Officials inside the State Department shared Blackwater's frustration at the information the Iraqi government was putting out to the press about the shooting. Some inside State believed that the Iraqi government was withholding information.

Secretary of State Condoleezza Rice telephoned Iraqi prime minister Nuri al-Maliki, expressing regret at the loss of life, explaining that she had ordered an internal investigation into the incident. It was the beginning of a delicate series of talks in which the United States would try to convince the Iraqis not to expel Blackwater. State Department spokesman Sean McCormack urged the press not to jump to conclusions, saying, "There was a firefight. We believe some innocent life was lost. Nobody wants to see that. But I can't tell you who was responsible for that."

Finding out who was responsible became the primary mission of several investigating bodies. Within a week after the shooting, some four separate investigations were announced. Secretary Rice decided to send a review team to Baghdad and asked Patrick Kennedy to lead it. Kennedy was working for John Negroponte at the United Nations at the time, but Rice knew that Kennedy had experience in Iraq from his days of working with Paul Bremer when he served as the head of the Coalition Provisional Authority. Kennedy had been an eyewitness when the contracting issue had first caused friction between the State Department and the Pentagon some three years earlier. Secretary Rice gave Kennedy and his three-man team a mandate to produce a "serious, probing, and comprehensive" report and offer recommendations on how to "protect our people while furthering our foreign policy objectives."

At Rice's direction, the team would *not* be made up entirely of State Department personnel. As Kennedy recalled, "She wanted to make sure the team had a broader perspective, so that the report would be unbiased, and so she asked for recommendations."

Kennedy tapped retired general George Joulwan, a former NATO supreme allied commander, Europe, who had taken a job in the private sector after retiring. Joulwan had also served on the Iraqi Security Forces Independent Assessment Commission headed by General Jones, the same commission that presented its findings to Congress that Iraq's Interior Ministry was a ministry in name only. Kennedy also tapped Ambassador Stapleton Roy, who, like Joulwan, had moved to the private sector after serving as a U.S. ambassador to China, Singapore, and Indonesia. Rounding out the team was Ambassador Eric Boswell, who had been the assistant secretary of state for diplomatic security and now worked for the director of national intelligence. Joulwan and Roy would have to negotiate the time away from their jobs. Meanwhile, the secretary wanted the rest of the team to deploy as soon as possible. "Eric Boswell and I were the two 'guvvies' who could get on a plane," said Kennedy. "[Secretary of State Rice] said on Wednesday, we want you to go, and we were on a plane on Saturday morning."

If Kennedy knew one thing from his previous experience in the country, it was that first reports were almost always wrong. The actual incident wasn't his official concern—plenty of other investigations were trying to sort it out—but he needed to examine the events leading up to it. There had been no Diplomatic Security officer in the advance team vehicles. There had been no cameras mounted on the vehicles that could help authorities understand how the events had unfolded. All of these were issues Kennedy and his team would consider.

There was just one thing Kennedy was fairly sure of as he arrived in Baghdad: ending the department's reliance on contractors wasn't an option. The State Department employed some 1,500 special agents around the world, and it couldn't send them all to Iraq. For the department to do everything it needed to do in Baghdad without Blackwater, it would need another 1,500 agents.

Not only was it not feasible, but the Iraq post was not a popular one within the State Department's 11,500-member foreign service sector. By November, Secretary Rice had to warn employees that they might be ordered to serve in the hardship post if there weren't more volunteers.

Kennedy and Boswell had already started working out a list of questions by the time Stapleton and Roy arrived. The four-man team settled into trailers that would serve as their living quarters behind the Republican Palace, while they worked by day in a makeshift office inside one of the palace's vast corridors. In all, they interviewed some sixty people. Some of those interviews required trips out in the field, protected by—whom else?—Blackwater.

At the end of every day, Kennedy and his team gathered in the palace corridor to give some structure to the interviews they'd conducted. "The biggest challenge was to figure out how to come up with a system to add rigor to the oversight process," said Kennedy. "We screen the people, we train the people, we certify the trainers, but clearly we needed another couple of layers on top of it, and that, I think, was the major issue."

Kennedy knew that it wasn't just Blackwater trying to defend itself against a host of questions in regards to the September 16 incident. The State Department was taking blame as well. People wanted to know why the department hadn't done more to oversee the work of contractors a long time ago. "The answer is, no one's ever done this before," answered Kennedy. "What is going on in Iraq now is unlike anything that I've ever read about. It's not Germany in 1946 or Japan in 1946. This is not Grenada, it's not Somalia, and so when you have something rolling out for which there is no precedent, you're inventing new processes as you go along."

It would take Kennedy's team close to two weeks to complete their report, but Secretary Rice wanted a first-blush opinion within ninety-six hours. Kennedy and Boswell responded with an interim report that suggested immediate changes to the way the State Department oversaw its contract force in Iraq. Some of the recommendations seemed to be little more than common sense, like making sure a special agent from the Bureau of Diplomatic Security accompanied all Blackwater teams. State would also start recording radio transmissions, instead of just monitoring them. They also recommended mounting video cameras in security vehicles, something that frustrated Prince when he heard it. His men had recommended this to the State Department two years earlier with no results. The vehicles used for Blackwater's contract with the Department of Defense, by contrast, already had vehicle-mounted cameras.

THE LEVEL OF FRUSTRATION among Blackwater executives hit a peak in the days and weeks after September 16. At least one executive inside the company wondered if Nisoor Square would be Blackwater's final chapter. Several executives had noticed a marked deterioration in the relationship with their biggest client, and they were coming to the realization that it was entirely possible that their contract wouldn't be renewed when it came up the following May. If the State Department were to cancel that contract, Blackwater's revenues would plunge at least by half.

Besides frustration, there was bitter disappointment that the State Department wasn't publicly taking any responsibility for what had happened. Blackwater executives were sure the version of events they had been told by their own employees was accurate, and some of them wondered how anyone could dare question it. Prince saw his men as patriots who had risked and lost their lives protecting State Department employees. He thought the State Department owed it to his people to give them the benefit of the doubt.

"I suppose it was part of the risk matrix that we had not really considered that they would have left us hanging that badly," said Prince. He insisted that if the roles were reversed, "We wouldn't leave them hanging that badly."

Another Blackwater employee echoed Prince's bitterness: "After the incident in Nisoor Square, what was written in the contract was really put to the test. What we were contracted to do was act at the direction of Diplomatic Security. We're doing what we're supposed to do under the contract with the Department of State, and then we would essentially turn to the Department of State and wait for their response and hear nothin' but crickets."

The Bureau of Diplomatic Security was the arm of the State Department responsible for providing the security needed for diplomats to do their jobs around the world. It was also the arm to which Blackwater reported. Greg Starr, the director of the division, was at the U.S. embassy in Kabul when he heard there had been an incident. By the time he got back to his office in Roslyn, Virginia, just days later, it was clear that he had a major problem on his hands. The regional security officers who worked for him had completed an initial report. Everyone realized that what had happened in Nisoor Square would need a more extensive investigation than what they were prepared to handle. While Blackwater was pressuring the department for some kind of public support, Starr was meeting with his own people, who were expressing serious concerns about what had occurred, and whether it rose to the level of a criminal act.

"I got the first report, and at that point, the seniors in the organization as a whole had concerns," recounted Starr. "The decision was made; we vetted it within the department, that this situation required more investigation."

Starr's division generally investigated every use of force in Iraq. Yet in this particular case, Starr and a few of his people had enough concerns that they made a trip across town to the Department of Justice. Getting to the bottom of the Nisoor Square incident would require the help of the FBI.

One Blackwater executive thought that DS and State were

throwing the company under the political train. "They can easily divert the attention by getting rid of us, and that's what they're doing. You know the old subway, the yellow line for the tracks? The subway's coming; Blackwater is about a foot past the line, and guess who's pushing us?"

THE STATE DEPARTMENT wasn't the only government department grappling with the fallout from Nisoor Square. By now the Department of Defense had some seven thousand armed private security contractors in Iraq, from a wide range of firms. Defense Secretary Robert Gates sent his own review team to Iraq to look at whether the Pentagon had enough accountability and oversight of its own contractors. During the week of the Nisoor Square incident, Gates closely watched the fallout unfold in the newspapers. He knew he needed to clarify his own department's stand on issues like accountability, visibility, and control of his contract teams in Iraq and Afghanistan. Gates directed Deputy Secretary of Defense Gordon England to call a Friday afternoon meeting.

As the Pentagon's deputy undersecretary of defense, Jack Bell had already spent a good deal of time working on the contractor issue. He had joined the department as the principal logistics official in 2005, bringing with him a mix of both military and private sector experience. He had helped design the system of overseeing contractors working both for Defense and for State. While he'd spent time in Iraq and Afghanistan, he was back in Washington when he heard there had been an incident in Nisoor Square. He had an immediate bad feeling about it. "I remember being aware of all of the other things that had gone on with our interaction with the State Department and the reputation that Blackwater had earned. I really thought when I heard about this

Nisoor Square incident that this was really going to push it over the edge in terms of the relationship with the Iraqis."

When England asked him what he thought about the contractor situation, Bell knew he couldn't give a quick answer. If a Pentagon contractor did something wrong on the job, what legal steps could be taken? While the Uniform Code of Military Justice (UCMJ) had been bandied around as a possible vehicle for investigations and prosecutions, there were significant legal concerns with whether it truly applied to nonmilitary personnel. It hadn't actually been used against anyone in the four and a half years since the war had begun.

England asked how quickly Bell and his team could be in Iraq. Bell suggested it would likely take the better part of two days to negotiate country clearance and book a flight. Fifteen minutes after the meeting, his phone rang. It was Secretary Gates's office. The secretary had made a plane available to Bell and his team. They would leave within twenty-four hours.

Bell loaded the plane with a team of three: his adviser, Colonel Daniel Williams, who had commanded the Third Infantry Division's Longbow Apache Battalion and had been in the lead unit in the march to liberate Iraq four years earlier; Ryan McCarthy, special assistant to the secretary of defense, who had also served with the Army Rangers and had been a leader of Delta Force before becoming a political appointee; and Joe Benkert, the principal deputy assistant secretary of defense for global security affairs. Before the team even landed, Colonel Williams was "prepping the battlefield," letting the commanders in Iraq know they were coming and what they wanted.

As the battlespace commander, General David Petraeus was already intimately familiar with the more sensitive aspects of the contracting issue. He had routed a request for legal clarification on the UCMJ accountability issue just one month earlier. It was a technicality, but a significant one. While many inside Defense knew the law was on the books, it had to be authorized for use by the secretary of defense himself. By Tuesday, September 25, Bell had a letter signed by the secretary authorizing the implementation of the UCMJ against civilian contractors accused of wrongdoing. It essentially meant that civilian contractors like those working for Prince could be court-martialed for their actions in Iraq. Some inside the Pentagon weren't even sure if it was constitutional, but everyone agreed that something like it was necessary. The Nisoor Square shooting was a hot topic among lawmakers in Washington, and everyone at the Pentagon knew they wouldn't be far behind the State Department in the chain of blame.

Bell and his team spent much of the first part of the trip meeting with top military officials. Many of them had already developed strong opinions about Blackwater and contractors in general. "They were very happy to have the chance to talk about this issue," recalled Bell. "[They were] happy to talk about their frustration with the lack of coherence and how the combat commanders could influence the operation of the contractors' movements."

Combat commanders had a long list of problems when it came to contractors on the battlefield. Teams of armed civilians were moving through battlespaces without warning. Contractors had run through checkpoints and shot at U.S. forces, and in one case a contractor convoy had even run a military unit off the road.

"A deputy commander who we should probably not name was forced off the road because he was shot at by contractors," said Colonel Williams. "For a career soldier like myself or for a former Marine like Secretary Bell, to have that kind of disregard for a division commander who commands fourteen thousand soldiers, by civilians, without any control is just totally unacceptable."

Oftentimes, there was no way for military commanders to know who the contractors were, or whom they worked for. The contractors were now approaching a one-to-one ratio with troops, and they were a different breed. Bell felt as if he had turned on a faucet of frustration in his interviews. "The combat commanders, the brigade commanders on the ground were saying we don't know who these guys are, we don't know when they come to our [zones], we don't know if they are driving down the road right into an operation we're trying to launch."

J. B. Burton was the commander of coalition forces in northwestern Baghdad on September 16. He oversaw two security districts that included Nisoor Square, with some five thousand troops under his command. There were 1.2 million Iraqis in his sector. It was a challenging job. Burton had to work with Iraqi Security Forces against any number of potential threats: al-Qaeda, militant militias, rampant crime, and sectarian tensions. His people knew the local streets, yet they had no idea that a Blackwater security detail was in the area that day.

"The type of conflict that we were in was built heavily on relationships and patterns and how you deal with human beings," said Burton. "I don't want to put myself in the position of those Blackwater men that day because I wasn't there, but every time I had gone through that square, there was a traffic jam. The sound of small arms fire was nothing new."

Regardless of whether the Blackwater men had come under attack or not, Burton would be left to clean up the damage. After he heard news of the shooting, he immediately dispatched teams to talk with local leaders. "Our number one priority," said Burton, "was to normalize relations, to lend a hand to our friends."

One recurring issue really bothered him. In close to one-third of the cases where his people got a call for a quick reaction force, it came from somebody he didn't even know was in his area. It put his men in the position of having to make a decision about whether to send a relief team to a potentially dangerous area without really knowing if the request was legitimate, or knowing whom they were being asked to assist. It was a stunning revelation for the military brass back home.

Secretary of Defense Gates wanted to assume control of all contractors on the battlefield, but the idea was met with fierce resistance from the State Department, which wanted to keep the military and diplomatic missions separate. A compromise was eventually reached to implement rules regarding contractor movements through military zones. From now on, regardless of whom they were working for, contractors would have to communicate better with the battlespace commander.

In Washington, Congressman Henry Waxman wanted answers of his own. He knew that Prince was a heavy contributor to Republican campaigns and was convinced that Blackwater had been given contracts based on insider handshakes, rather than competitive bidding, something Prince always denied. Democrats were livid that more hadn't been done in Congress to regulate the control of contractors on the battlefield while the Republicans were in control.

Waxman's office sent a letter to Prince asking him to testify at a hearing scheduled for early October. The office also released a scathing report that included a litany of allegations against the company: everything from lax management at the Fallujah bridge incident in 2004 to the fatal crash of the Blackwater plane in Afghanistan. Prince would have to answer to all of it himself.

When the letter arrived at Blackwater, some of the company's senior advisers were concerned, not so much because of Prince's lack of experience on the Hill, but because they were worried that if he got mad enough, he might just come over the table at those questioning him. But Prince had made up his mind. He wouldn't send Cofer Black or Rob Richer, or any of the other people in his employ who had experience testifying before congressional committees. This time he would go.

Having a pretty good idea of what he was in for, Prince hired Washington attorneys Steve Ryan and Beth Nolan to help him prepare. "I went through every incident report from the previous years," recalled Prince. "I went through the contract and the training requirements for each guy going out on the contract." He and his team spent the better part of a week role-playing, anticipating the questions he might be asked to try and throw him off guard. In his mind, Prince was preparing for a show trial where Democrats would try and set a perjury trap. He was determined not to fall in it.

It didn't help that as the preparations continued, details of the Nisoor Square shooting continued to trickle out of Iraq in the form of stories of the survivors. They were heart wrenching. One Iraqi account described a Blackwater guard shooting and killing the driver of a vehicle, his body slumping over the wheel. As the car continued to move in the direction of the convoy, the contractors unleashed a barrage of firepower. The man's mother, who sat beside him, screamed before she, too, was silenced by bullets. By several accounts, the guards fired a grenade-type explosive into the vehicle. There were also stories of the youngest victims. One of those killed that day was reported to be a nine-year-old Iraqi boy.

As the Iraqis gave their accounts to investigators and the media, U.S. sources also continued to leak information about the investigation. Some claimed that one or more of the Black-water guards called for a cease-fire after the shooting began and that there were already Blackwater helicopters overhead. In the chaos, some of the Iraqis on the ground thought the helicopters also fired at the civilians, something Blackwater denied. But the incident was still under investigation by the FBI, as it would be for quite some time.

As Prince prepared for his testimony, some inside the company believed that the State Department was trying to keep them from providing information to the committee. In a series of phone calls and in a letter sent to Blackwater dated September 20, a State Department contracting officer offered a firm reminder of the language in the contract between Blackwater and State that dealt with contract records and the disclosure of information, citing Section H.7 H–020, Safeguarding of Information.

> *The Contractor and its employees shall exercise the utmost discretion in regard to all matters relating to their duties and functions. They shall not communicate to any person any information known to them by reason of their performance of services under this contract which has not been made public, except in the necessary performance of their duties or upon written authorization of the Contracting Officer. All documents and records (including photographs) generated during the performance of work under this contract shall be for the sole use of and become the exclusive property of the U.S. Government. Furthermore, no article, book, pamphlet, recording, broadcast, speech, television appearance, film or photograph concerning any aspect of work performed under this contract shall be published or disseminated through any media without the prior written authorization of the Contracting Officer.*

These obligations do not cease upon the expiration or termination of this contract. The Contractor shall include the substance of this provision in all contracts of employment and in all subcontracts hereunder.

The Diplomatic Security office denied that the reminder was an attempt to keep Prince from answering the committee's questions. Prince saw it differently: "They were trying to get us to hold back on all kinds of stuff." In any event, Prince was determined to tell his side of the story. In a way, he was happy to answer Waxman's request to appear. He believed he could set the record straight once and for all.

CHAPTER 9

The Secretary and the Prince

PRINCE GOT UP EARLY on the morning of October 2, 2007. After preparing for more than a week, he was ready to testify before the House Committee on Oversight and Government Reform. Maybe after today the Democratic members of the committee would see him more as he saw himself, as a true American patriot. At least, so he hoped—but he didn't hold his breath in expectation. His testimony would be carried live on C-Span, and virtually everyone he knew would be watching. Even his mother back home in Michigan began the day with a prayer for her son.

The night before, Prince had gotten calls of support from old family friends like Chuck Colson. He also got a call from another old friend who knew better than most what he was about to go through. Oliver North had spent lots of time in the congressional hot seat in connection with the Iran–Contra affair under President Ronald Reagan. He assured Erik he'd do just fine and wished him the best.

In a conference room with his lawyers and most trusted

friends and advisers, Prince went over final preparations. There
had been a last-minute curveball. Because it was still investigating the incident as a potential crime, the Department of Justice
asked Prince not to talk about the Nisoor Square shooting. Once
again, he was muzzled on the one story that mattered most.

Gary Jackson had flown up from Moyock to be with the boss
on the big day. Prince's media adviser Paul Behrends and Blackwater's own chaplain, the Reverend George Pucherelli, were also
there. On the one hand, Jackson was relieved that Prince would
finally be able to set the record straight on some of the misinfor-
mation circulated in the media. On the other, he felt bad for his
boss, who had worked so hard to stay out of the media glare, only
now to be squarely positioned in the middle of it.

"I know he wasn't comfortable doing that, but there was absolutely no choice at that point in time," said Jackson. Committee
chair Henry Waxman didn't want to see another company vice
president or lawyer. This time he wanted answers from the man
at the top.

As Prince and his team went over the last-minute changes,
his attorney, Steve Ryan, tried to reassure him. "He said, 'Erik,
this is the low point for the company,'" recalled Prince. "'You are
about to start its return. Go out there and be ready.'"

As he entered the hearing room with a close haircut and dark
athletic-cut suit, Prince looked more like an all-American boy
than the head of one of the country's most controversial private
military firms. Seated on the floor between him and the committee members was a row of photographers firing off a rapid series
of flashbulbs.

This was the day Congressman Waxman and several other
Democrats had been waiting for. As he called the House Committee on Oversight and Government Reform to order, Waxman

reminded them of why they were there: to take a harder look at private security contracting in Iraq and Afghanistan. Not only was Waxman focusing on the recent events involving Blackwater, but he was also looking for answers about how the Department of Defense had managed to raise a vast private army in Iraq without congressional approval.

"Over the past twenty-five years, a sophisticated campaign has been waged to privatize government services. The theory is that corporations can deliver government services better and at a lower cost than the government," Waxman began. "Over the last six years, this theory has been put into practice. The result is that privatization has exploded. For every taxpayer dollar spent on federal programs, over forty cents now goes to private contractors. Our government now outsources even the oversight of the outsourcing."

The committee was also looking to answer basic questions about Blackwater: Was the company helping or hurting U.S. efforts in Iraq? Was the government doing enough to hold Blackwater accountable for alleged misconduct? And just how much money was Blackwater being paid by U.S. taxpayers?

Waxman laid out the company's phenomenal growth in financial terms, telling the committee that Blackwater had just over $200,000 in federal contracts in 2000, and that the company had earned more than $1 billion in just seven years. It was a rough figure that apparently included both classified and public contracts; indeed, it was the first authoritative public statement by anyone in the government, much less at Blackwater, to at least estimate the company's bottom line. It was a stunning number for a company owned solely by one man.

Waxman laid out the ways in which the larger issue of contracting was proving to put an operational strain on the gov-

ernment that was paying for their services. "Defense Secretary
Gates testified about this problem last week. He said Blackwater
charges the government so much, that it can lure highly trained
soldiers out of our forces to work for them," said Waxman. "He
is now taking the unprecedented step of considering whether to
ask our troops to sign a noncompete agreement to prevent the
U.S. military from becoming a taxpayer-funded training program
for private contractors."

He went on to discuss the Christmas Eve shooting, the State
Department's role in determining how much money to pay the
family of the slain Iraqi guard, and the decision to allow the contractor to fly home hours after the shooting. He cited messages
back and forth between the State Department and senior-level
Blackwater employees. "It's hard to read these e-mails and not
come to the conclusion that the State Department is acting as
Blackwater's enabler," said Waxman.

The congressman also acknowledged the families of the Fallujah victims who had come to Washington to see Prince testify
in person. They had already testified before the committee eight
months earlier, complaining to the members of Congress that the
company was stonewalling them over the deaths. Donna Zovko
sat in the audience, remembering her husband's comment from
years earlier, that Prince resembled their son. To her, Prince had
become not only the man who refused to answer her questions,
but the man who refused to meet with her at all once the lawsuit
had been filed.

"It had been so long since I had seen Erik Prince, and I wanted
to see him, and I wanted to see how truthful he would be about
testifying," recalled Zovko. "Sometimes you can see it on the TV,
but it's not the same as when the person is in front of you; it gives
you more closure." The person in front of her that morning wasn't

the same Erik Prince she had met years earlier in her son's dining room. This was a man hardened, determined, and prepared for the mission ahead. "I didn't know what to expect," said Zovko, "but I wanted that human part of him to come out; I wanted him to be that Erik, who actually was human and cared."

Waxman addressed the families directly, saying, "I know many of you believe that Blackwater has been unaccountable to anyone in our government. I want you to know that Blackwater will be accountable today."

Prince knew he was in for a tough day. As he rose before the committee, raising his right hand to be sworn in, the flashbulbs again lit up the chamber. They didn't stop, even as he began his opening statement, his voice shaking.

"After almost five years in active service as a U.S. Navy SEAL, I founded Blackwater in 1997. I wanted to offer the military and law enforcement communities assistance by providing expert instruction and world-class training venues. Ten years later, Blackwater trains approximately 500 members of the United States military and law enforcement agencies every day," Prince read.

He went on to describe his company as simply a patriotic organization that had answered the call of duty.

"After 9/11, when the U.S. began its stabilization efforts in Afghanistan and then Iraq, the United States government called upon Blackwater to fill a need for protective services in hostile areas. Blackwater responded immediately. We are extremely proud of answering that call in supporting our country," Prince read, adding that "Blackwater personnel supporting our overseas missions are all military and law enforcement veterans, many of whom have recent military deployments. No individual ever protected by Blackwater has ever been killed or seriously injured. There is no better evidence of the skill and dedication of these men." It was a claim that elided the plane crash in Afghanistan—technically, his men were not performing security duties in that case.

Prince informed the committee that thirty of his men had been killed on the job and closed by assuring them that Blackwater shared their interest in ensuring accountability in the industry. With that, some four hours of back-and-forth began. The Republican members of the committee took it easy on him, thanking Prince for his service to his country, while the Democrats were probing, accusatory, and focused repeatedly on the company's transgressions.

Waxman began with the crash of Blackwater Flight 61 in Afghanistan three years earlier. Both the Army and Air Force Task Force and the National Transportation Safety Board had launched investigations, and the NTSB had found that two of the Presidential Airways men involved had acted unprofessionally. "The report found that the pilots were unfamiliar with the route, deviated almost immediately after takeoff, and failed to maintain adequate terrain clearance," said Waxman, posing the question of whether Prince's men were the "cowboys" they were often described to be.

"Anytime you have an accident, it's an accident; something could have been done better," Prince retorted. "It is truly rugged, Alaska-style bush flying."

Waxman read an e-mail from the company's site manager in Afghanistan sent to a company vice president before the crash, detailing that the company hired pilots who it knew didn't meet the experience requirements of the job.

Waxman read aloud: "By necessity, the initial group hired to support the Afghanistan operation did not meet the criteria identified in e-mail traffic and had some background and experience shortfalls overlooked in favor of getting the requisite number of personnel onboard to start up the contract."

It sounded a lot like the accusations that the Fallujah victims' families had made against the company: shortcuts had been taken that jeopardized lives.

Prince responded by saying, "I believe the Air Force investigated the incident, and they found that it was pilot error; it was not due to corporate error that caused the problem—the mistake that had crashed the aircraft."

Prince did his best to offer his own sound bites, much as Oliver North had once managed to do during contentious congressional hearings over the Iran–Contra affair. At one point, he offered a prepared anecdote: "I have to say, my proudest professional moment was about a year and a half ago, I spoke at the National War College. After my speech, a colonel, full bird colonel, came up to me. And he said, 'You know, I just came back from a brigade command in Baghdad.' As his guys were driving around the city, on the tops of their dashboards of their Humvees were the Blackwater call signs and the frequencies, because his soldiers knew that, if they got in trouble, the Blackwater guys would come for them. They would come to their aid and assist them, medevac them, and help them out of a tough spot."

But Waxman was ready with his own sound bite. He quoted a senior U.S. military official that "Blackwater's actions are creating resentment among Iraqis that, quote, 'may be worse than Abu Ghraib,' end quote." As Waxman brought up more quotes from members of the military about contractors behaving badly, Prince had an answer ready.

"I can tell you there's 170-some security companies operating through Iraq. We get painted with a very broad brush on a lot of the stuff they do," said Prince. "On an almost weekly basis, we get a contact from someone in DoD that says, 'Oh, three Black-water guys were just taken hostage here. Four guys were killed there. Oh, you were involved in a shooting over there,'" only to find out it wasn't Blackwater personnel at all.

The committee also tried to drill down on the issue of just how much money Blackwater was making off its roughly fifty U.S. government contracts. But Prince wasn't about to give them what they wanted. Testifying that while he wasn't interested in disclosing Blackwater's full financials, Prince said the company maintained a profit margin of around 10 percent.

Congressman Peter Welch asked Prince to walk through the math. "If Blackwater had $1 billion in contracts since the war began in 2003, and there's a 10 percent profit margin, that's $100 million in profit, is it not?"

Prince refused a direct answer, saying only that his company had also lost money on expensive assets like little bird helicopters that they had not been able to insure.

At least by the end of the hearing Prince knew that Black-water wasn't in the line of fire alone. Waxman closed by saying, "The committee's investigation raises as many questions about the State Department's oversight of Blackwater as it does about Blackwater itself."

After four hours, Prince walked out of the hearing room confident that he had answered his critics. His only doubt was whether the "liberal-leaning media" would feel the same.

THE MORNING AFTER Prince testified, he woke up to news of an unexpectedly positive story involving his men in Iraq. A convoy carrying the Polish ambassador to Baghdad had come under attack by insurgents using explosively formed projectiles.

There were injuries, and one man was killed. Coalition forces needed to evacuate the ambassador by air, but the military could not respond immediately. Blackwater was monitoring the radio calls for help and decided to send its own team. Dan Laguna, Blackwater's aviation manager, was among those who responded. He maneuvered the company helicopter onto the street where the ambassador was trapped. The ambassador's team was able to help put their boss onboard so he could be flown to a hospital for treatment of his serious burns.

The grateful ambassador would thank the Blackwater team three months later at a ceremony in their honor, by pinning Poland's Silver and Bronze Star medals onto the shirts of eighteen honorees. It was the first time the awards had been bestowed on foreigners since World War II.

But on the day of the rescue, Prince was again frustrated. While the media had no problem reporting the details of the September 16 incident, there was very little mention of this story. Once again, Blackwater couldn't trumpet the issue publicly, without violating the terms of its contract with the State Department. Prince was starting to see the true dilemma of running a private company under government rules: his company was fast becoming radioactive, and there wasn't much he could do about it.

In the aftermath of his testimony, the media sharpened their claws. Thanks in part to a press release that Waxman's office had offered prior to the hearing, there was more fodder than ever before. Prince huddled for the better part of two days with his top staff to come up with a strategy to defend the company both in public and in the face of the FBI investigation of Nisoor Square. "Man," said Prince, "we're getting the crap kicked out of us. We've got to do something."

"In spite of the hearing, the media started drifting back incredibly negative," recalled Paul Behrends. "It was almost like they went to a different hearing, so the decision was to defend the company because it was not any longer about keeping a contract, it was about defending our reputation, and the reputation of the company, because we felt like they were trying to destroy it."

Prince's team felt they had little choice but to take matters into their own hands with a public relations blitz. There was talk about who would be the face of the campaign, but no one in the company had significant media experience; certainly none had ever taken on a task like this. The media had been requesting interviews with Prince himself, and eventually the decision was made that there was no better person to do it.

The move posed a great risk given the terms of Blackwater's contract with State. But if things continued the way they were going, that contract might never be renewed. Some in the company estimated that the State Department contract constituted some 50 percent of Blackwater's business. Others close to Prince put the number much higher, closer to 80 percent. So the decision to go public was fraught with risk, but Prince felt he had no choice. When Blackwater let the State Department know of its plans, it wasn't to ask permission.

It was a Wednesday when the decision was finalized. Prince would book major interviews, one by one, and present the facts as he saw them. "Get *60 Minutes* here on Friday," said Prince. "They can come on Thursday and shoot their B-roll stuff. I'll be there on Friday, but they have to air it on Sunday. Give them a very short window so they have no time to screw around on it."

After Prince had kept quiet for so long, producers and interviewers jumped at the chance to talk with him. The *Washington Post* interviewed him on Thursday. He taped an interview with

PBS's Charlie Rose on Friday. His first live television appearance would come on CNN on Sunday during the day, followed by *60 Minutes* that evening. The next morning Prince was on a plane to Chicago, where he would sit down with NBC's Matt Lauer. He flew back to Virginia and boarded another of his planes for the short trip down to Moyock to spend the day showing the Blackwater campus to a CNN crew. He joked as he drove them around the property, asking, "Is this what your liberal-leaning friends want to see?"

The point of the media blitz had been to convince the country that Blackwater had done nothing wrong and that it was led by a true American patriot. The plan called for a sudden flurry of appearances, and then, just as suddenly, to go quiet again. Prince would use the blitz to do what he wasn't allowed to do in the hearing: talk about September 16. In nearly every interview he asked people not to rush to judgment regarding his men or what happened in Nisoor Square that day, and he stood behind his employees by touting their professional credentials. He insisted that he had seen photographic proof that the Blackwater vehicles had come under attack. If anyone did do anything wrong, he said, he would support prosecution, but all of that would have to wait for the outcome of the pending FBI investigation, which would take quite some time.

Prince also repeated one of his favorite points: he had not gone looking for security work, he said; his company had merely stepped up when the U.S. government needed it to. He wanted to paint an image of himself not as a rich monopolist, but a simple patriot. With future business in mind, however, he also used the public stage to remind people that smaller, efficient companies like his could do what international governments had failed to do in places like Darfur.

The stories and interviews rolled out, and Prince did succeed in making his case at each appearance, with only minimal challenges from most of his interviewers. Yet as the blogosphere took over, those same interviews only seemed to invigorate concern over the use of private security contractors with no clear chain of effective accountability. Prince was the hook for a much larger story: a shadow army made up of unaccountable private contractors was being lavishly funded by the U.S. government. Some executives at the company understood what they were seeing: Blackwater was the unwitting poster child of the industry, and they were paying a heavy price for failing to engage a media strategy years earlier. Gary Jackson was among the most vocal critics.

"I believe the media is probably the greatest danger to the United States of America more than anything else," said Jackson. "They are more dangerous than the terrorists, more dangerous than illegal aliens, they are more dangerous than any other thing the U.S. has to worry about." It's the kind of off-the-cuff talk that just fuels his critics' fire.

Jackson had gotten into the habit of rising early to scan blogs and the Web sites of major news organizations. He wondered how an American was supposed to know what's going on in the world, when he could find several different news outlets covering the same story with such radically different takes.

Prince's former SEAL buddy and now Blackwater vice president Chris Burgess expressed similar frustration. "You have the government, the DoD's perspective versus the State Department's perspective, the Iraqi government's perspective versus the U.S. government's perspective, and how we've kind of been used as this tool for everybody to bat each other over the head. You know, Congress and the executive branch and that kind of thing."

In their eyes, Blackwater was a punching bag for everyone,

THE SECRETARY AND THE PRINCE

from the evil media to the self-interested government agencies to the untrustworthy Iraqis. Jackson was angry that the hits in the media just kept coming, even after Prince had tried to personally deflect the criticism. "He had spent many years trying to stay out of the public eye," said Jackson. "It hasn't been a pretty time."

Prince and his advisers nonetheless decided they had done what they'd set out to do, and now it was time to get back to business. Behrends explained that the company had no interest in keeping Prince in the media's glare. "We made our point and went back to running the company, and we've been focused on core competencies of excellent service and all that stuff. We didn't take our eye off the ball. We're not trying to run a political campaign or a media campaign."

ONE ISSUE Henry Waxman continued to drill down on concerned Blackwater's relationship with the State Department. Howard Krongard, the State Department's inspector general, faced questions of whether he hindered investigations into the company. Waxman wanted to know whether Krongard had refused to cooperate with investigators looking into alleged weapons smuggling actions by Blackwater employees. Krongard denied the charge, telling Waxman that he had "made one of my best investigators available to help assistant U.S. attorneys in North Carolina in their investigation into alleged smuggling of weapons into Iraq by a contractor."

It was the first public acknowledgment of the investigation into whether Blackwater had smuggled its weapons into Iraq illegally. As is typical with ongoing investigations, the U.S. attorneys refused to comment. The company insisted it broke no laws.

Waxman seemed more concerned with the fact that Howard

Krongard happened to be the brother of Buzzy Krongard, the same Buzzy Krongard who was the executive director of the CIA in 2001 when Blackwater got its first black contract, a secret contract, of which the details are not available to the public. After leaving the CIA, Buzzy had gone on to serve on Blackwater's board of advisers, a board that had no real authority or hand in day-to-day operations. Prince had created it, in his words, to "make the company look more normal." But to Waxman, it looked abnormal, more like a conflict of interest. The brothers both adamantly denied there was any concerted effort to protect Blackwater.

Congress was hardly the only branch of government making significant accusations against the company. The Internal Revenue Service was also on Blackwater's case, saying the company's classification of its hired workers as "independent contractors" wasn't justified. As independent contractors, those working for the company would be responsible for paying their own federal and state taxes. Waxman suggested that the classification was a violation of tax law and that Blackwater may have defrauded the government of millions of dollars. The company scoffed at the accusation, calling it "groundless."

There was yet one more investigation still to come, and this one felt personal. The International Peace Operations Organization (IPOA) was an industry-wide umbrella organization, part lobbying vehicle, part voluntary ethics regulator. Blackwater was a founding member, and the company had taken an active role in helping to define many of the standards the IPOA set for the industry. So Gary Jackson didn't take it well when the IPOA tried to launch its own investigation into Blackwater after September 16. The IPOA called the company before its Standards and Ethics Committee. Jackson saw it as a slap in the face.

"We helped them write the code of ethics," said Jackson. "Blackwater was instrumental in putting all of those pieces in place. When the rubber hit the road, I felt that they did not stick with the plan."

Jackson was so outraged and disappointed by the investigation that he decided enough was enough. The company abruptly withdrew its support and membership. "I think they should have stepped out there loud and clear and said we know this company, they've been with us for years, they helped us write the ethics and the standards," said Jackson.

The IPOA insisted it was following the rules and regulations laid out for all of its members. Blackwater wouldn't get special treatment.

AMID ALL THE PULLING and pushing, as Erik Prince looked ahead to the State Department's upcoming spring decision about whether or not to renew Blackwater's contract, he had one source of leverage. The company's helicopters, vital means of transportation to and from reconstruction meetings, were retrofitted with the equipment needed to fly in hostile areas. The State Department leased those helicopters from Blackwater under a separate contract. Prince made it clear that Blackwater's contracts with State were an all-or-nothing deal. Cancel the security contract; lose the use of the helicopters as well.

After nearly three weeks of being on the ground in Iraq, Ambassador Pat Kennedy and his team were ready to fly back to Washington to deliver their findings to Secretary Rice. The team arrived back in Washington on a Thursday. By Friday evening they were sitting down with the secretary in a conference room near her office, inside the main State Department building in

Washington. The team recommended that an assistant State Department regional security officer accompany every motorcade involving contract security personnel; that the Worldwide Personal Protective Services contract be amended to provide for contractors to engage Arabic language staff to be used in convoys; that additional training for cultural awareness be offered for diplomatic and military procedures; that ground rules surrounding the use of deadly force be more sharply defined; and that video-recording equipment be installed in every security vehicle.

The secretary agreed with all of the recommendations. But there was more: Kennedy's team also wanted to create a Go Team, a group that would act as the first State Department investigators on the scene of an incident. They would go to the scene where weapons had been discharged and gather information to assist with preparing a comprehensive report of the details surrounding the event. The team would work with both the Iraqis and the U.S. military personnel assigned to the area where the incident occurred. Rather than rely on Blackwater's reports about its own activities, State needed its own investigators. Had such a team existed at the time of the Nisoor Square incident, they may have had a far easier time collecting evidence. Blackwater would still be a major presence in Iraq, but at least the government would take back responsibility for monitoring and investigating its contractors—no longer would contractors be in the position of monitoring themselves.

JUST WEEKS AFTER Prince testified on the Hill, Secretary Rice herself was called before the House Committee on Oversight and Government Reform. While the focus of the hearing was largely on corruption issues in Iraq, there was no way the secretary would leave the room without addressing her department's continued use of Blackwater. The Iraqi government was still demanding that the company be expelled. The department had just briefly suspended Blackwater convoys in the days after the incident occurred, and they were already back on the job. Some in the military were perplexed. Many Democrats in Congress were suspicious. The Iraqis were furious.

Rice did her best to address the concerns. She knew that if State was going to retain control over its own contractors and not lose that control to the military, there would have to be a closer working relationship with the Department of Defense. Secretary Gates and Secretary Rice had already talked about the issue by phone and had assigned their top deputies to come up with another set of recommendations focused on better coordination and communication.

One of the first questions Secretary Rice was asked about Blackwater before the House committee was also one of the most direct. Why had it taken four years for the State Department to take steps ensuring better oversight of its contractors, when a strong warning had come two and a half years earlier? At that time, according to a cable from Baghdad to the State Department back in Washington, a Blackwater team fired at a civilian car as it approached a motorcade. One Iraqi was killed, and two were injured. The State Department's own investigation found that the Blackwater personnel acted inappropriately, considering the threat involved. The State Department asked for the men to be fired and sent home. Rice declined to get into the specifics of the incident. All she could say was that the steps taken most recently, thanks to the Kennedy commission, were an effort to remedy the situation. She asked that legislation be passed so that appropriate actions could in fact be taken in situations like these.

Critics on the committee retorted that the State Department had done almost nothing to address the company's tactics, while continuing to pay Blackwater more than $800 million.

PRINCE WAS DISGUSTED: the media were against him. The Democrats were against him. The State Department was doing nothing for him. Blackwater had critics at Defense. His company name had become a symbol of out-of-control cowboys and profiteers. Yet it was not in Prince's nature to stew quietly; instead, he channeled his energy into plowing forward, pushing for more contracts, planning expansion, building new aircraft, and rushing around to shore up his friendly contacts behind the scenes.

The U.S. ambassador in Iraq, Ryan Crocker, said he still held his Blackwater guards in high regard. President Bush told a newspaper reporter that private firms like Blackwater provided a valuable service. Prince needed to get out in the field to work his contacts. Afghanistan would bring a welcome change of itinerary from the issues in Iraq.

Presidential Airways still had a nearly $100 million contract there to provide airlift support for the Department of Defense. Prince also had men working for the CIA in Afghanistan on the classified contract helping to operate the agency's secret locations. That contract had been extended several times since it was first awarded back in 2002.

It was time to get on a plane and head east.

Just two weeks before his trip, there were leaked reports that the FBI was coming to the conclusion that many, if not all, of the shootings that took place on September 16 in Nisoor Square were unjustified. Investigators were reportedly looking at one Blackwater guard in particular, though it was not clear that he could be prosecuted. Investigators had arrived at the scene weeks after the event, and statements by the Blackwater contractors had been given to State Department investigators under the promise that they would not be used in a criminal investigation.

As Prince packed his bags for Kabul, he had two missions in mind: to make sure his customers were still happy and to test the waters for just how much future business the Nisoor Square incident may have cost him.

CHAPTER 10

Mission in Afghanistan

IF ERIK PRINCE was tired from the fourteen-hour flight to Dubai, he didn't show it. At age thirty-eight, he still had boyish energy. He strode off the plane in late November 2007 with a small entourage after the first leg of a longer journey to Kabul and elsewhere in Afghanistan. Prince traveled with a personal bodyguard who had served as a U.S. Army Ranger, something he thought necessary after his employees at Total Intelligence Solutions had picked up chatter on Web sites suggesting that terrorist-linked groups wanted to kill him. He also traveled on this particular trip with a professor from the Washington-based Institute of World Politics. The professor, Michael Waller, had met Prince years earlier through Representative Dana Rohrabacher. In the days after the Nisoor Square incident, Waller had approached Prince with a proposal: Prince should write a book. He would ghostwrite it for him. Waller also served as an editor for an online publication called Serviam. He was very industry-friendly and eager to work with Prince.

Prince thought an alliance might offer a convenient way to broaden his media strategy by laying out a manifesto, telling his side of the story in his own (ghosted) words. He had even settled on a title: *We Are Blackwater*. The attractions of a book were obvious: Prince wouldn't be limited to answering the questions he was asked by reporters and senators. He could control the message. A book deal with Regnery, a publisher known for its conservative politics, would be announced in February 2008. Yet once again, the State Department would put its foot down and kill the deal, at least for the time being.

The flight from Dubai to Kabul didn't leave for several hours, so the group headed to a hotel often used as a resting point for the hundreds of contractors moving in and out of Iraq and Afghanistan. The upscale hotel offered the group a chance to recharge with a meal and a few hours' sleep. As Prince perused a menu and pondered pasta, he went over the details of the week ahead. The group would be met by a Blackwater security team in Kabul. They would be escorted from one meeting to another with employees of the Department of State, the CIA, and the Department of Defense. Prince wanted to know how his company was being perceived half a world away from the Washington media. In addition to the contracts with the CIA and with Defense for airlifting supplies to troops, Blackwater had guards working for the Department of State at the U.S. embassy annex in Kabul. Finally, his men trained Afghans for border patrol and narcotics interdiction. All four contracts needed to be handled with care, given the new controversies the company faced.

Prince had realistic hopes of gaining some new business. Clashes between coalition forces and the Taliban along the country's borders had been brutal, and Prince was already in the business of training Afghans to stop the illicit flow of drugs that was believed to be funding the insurgency. Surely more could be done. Afghanistan was a big market for Blackwater, and Prince hoped he could expand his business on this trip.

The five-hour stopover in Dubai was interesting in its own right. Dubai had become a well-used stop on the road to Iraq for many of the 160,000 private military contractors now working in the country. Some 48,000 of that total number were private security contractors, like Prince's men. Those were people who needed to get in and out of the country several times a year, depending on the length of their rotations. They needed airline tickets, a place to stay. It had turned many upscale Dubai hotels into resting points for the eclectic group of men drawn to that kind of work. Dubai is the economic gem of the United Arab Emirates, and the city's rapidly expanding skyline was proof of the billions of investment dollars flowing in. The United Arab Emirates had boasted a double-digit growth rate and planned to sustain it for some time to come. Prince mused aloud about buying his own building in the city.

The two-and-a-half-hour flight to Kabul was packed with a combination of contractors, military types, and some random folk who looked as if they had stepped off a movie set. In fact, just a few rows behind Prince sat a bald actor who had played a cameo role in an *Indiana Jones* movie.

For Prince, the trip was not just about clients; it was also a chance to meet some of the eclectic, modern-day soldiers of fortune who worked under him. Prince and his companions were met on the ground by a two-vehicle Blackwater team led by former FBI special agent Ricky "C.T." Chambers. After his earlier work for the bureau investigating the embassy bombings in Nairobi and Dar es Salaam, he had become Blackwater's regional director of training in Afghanistan in 2003 for the Drug Enforce-

ment Agency and Afghan narcotics interdiction contracts, as well
as the Afghan border police training programs. C.T. knew everyone in Kabul. He liked his job, particularly because he was one
of the few men who could live in Afghanistan with his wife, a
British beauty whom he'd met years earlier during his FBI days
in Kenya. M.C., as she liked to be called, now ran Blackwater's
administrative efforts in the country, including the oversight of
some forty local nationals.

C.T. greeted the boss with a handshake and a bulletproof vest.
There had been a suicide bombing in the capital that morning,
and at least a few people were killed. It happened not far from
Blackwater's safe houses, and some of the employees had gone
to the roof to get a better look at the huge plume of smoke rising
from the site of the attack. Suicide bombings were becoming
more common in the capital, even in broad daylight in crowded
areas where security was present. Taliban insurgents were wiring
up Afghans who were mentally or physically disabled, the under-
privileged who would sit along the side of the busy streets hoping
for someone to drop money into their laps. When a U.S. convoy
or other acceptable target got close enough, militants would remotely detonate their victims.

Prince put on his vest for a five-minute ride to the other side
of the airport. One of his planes was being prepared to take him
to the country's largest airfield, where his own pilots were based.
There were armed security guards in each of the two Blackwater
SUVs, but Prince kept his own Glock on the seat next to him.
He kept his eyes open as the convoy moved along the crowded
Kabul streets, where fresh meat carcasses hung out to dry and
barefooted kids played in the narrow, dust-ridden alleyways. He
particularly watched for teenagers on cell phones, standing on
corners. He had seen intelligence information suggesting teens

were being paid by insurgents to scout out Western convoys and report their coordinates for a possible attack.

Once safely inside the airport's perimeter, Prince and his team made their way to the Blackwater plane sitting on the tarmac. He greeted his pilots and asked how things were going. They assured him that the DoD was happy with the job they were doing. Despite the crash of Blackwater Flight 61 into the side of a mountain two years earlier, Presidential Airways had continued to sign contracts with the Pentagon several times since then, including a $91 million-a-year contract to provide air support in Guam. Prince's company had eight Cessna aircraft in Afghanistan, working for the Department of Defense. His men flew everything from drug eradication missions to bundle drops. Many of them were high-risk flights from forward operating bases in the countryside.

The flight to Bagram Air Field, just twenty-seven miles north of Kabul, was quick and easy. The base is surrounded by remnants of the Soviet occupation of Afghanistan in the 1980s: rusted-out tanks and spent ammunition litter the perimeter, as do hundreds of land mines. Nongovernmental organizations had roped off vast sections of land around Bagram to begin the painstaking process of demining.

In the early days after the U.S. invasion in 2001, Special Operations command officers along with troops from the Tenth Mountain Division and the Eighty-second Airborne Division used Bagram as a strategic operating base. Recent years had seen the arrival of thousands of international peacekeepers, contractors, and journalists. One entire section of the base had become known as "contractor village."

Between the NATO mission at Bagram and the vast number of contractors employed by the military, space was at a premium, so Prince's employees had been creative with what they had. They showed the boss how they had turned regular cargo containers into working storage facilities for spare parts. They had even turned one of them into a makeshift welding shop. Prince finished his tour of the Blackwater area by visiting the company's small office and pilots' quarters, made from plywood. They called them "B huts," and for contractors and troops alike, they were home.

Prince disappeared for a meeting with a State Department representative, then flew off to visit a CIA operating post. Everywhere he went, he was treated like a celebrity, posing for pictures with military men and Blackwater employees.

If there was an architect of the U.S. invasion of Afghanistan, it had been the Central Intelligence Agency. While Prince had used his connection to A. B. "Buzzy" Krongard, the former executive director of the CIA, to get his first black contract for security work, the agency had continued to renew Blackwater's work, even after Krongard had left.

At the secret CIA post, Prince met with a handful of his men who had come to greet him. Several of them looked as if they had walked out of an *X-Files* convention: long hair, plaid flannel shirts, and baggy pants worn much further down than pants were meant to be worn. Prince, in keeping with his conservative upbringing, gave some of them a hard time about their appearance, but they insisted it was what worked best among the local population. Prince's men had apparently made the CIA happy, providing static security and performing unknown other tasks. But some in the European Parliament suspected that Prince's Presidential Airways had operated rendition flights for the CIA, and said so in a report. An attorney for Prince pressed the European

Parliament for proof to support such a claim, but proof never materialized. The attorney insisted the statements in the report were false and demanded a correction. While the possibility of Prince's companies taking part seemed plausible, Prince denied it ever happened.

Prince wrapped up the conversation with his men after about twenty minutes and reboarded the CASA for the flight back to Kabul. Blackwater's safe houses there were located right around the corner from the local headquarters of the "OGA." It was one of the more affectionate terms for the "other government agency" more commonly known as the CIA. Some of his contractors would mingle with the government employees in the evening at the gym.

Two of the men guarding Prince during his trip had already spent years in the contracting business. Philip "Buster" McTigue knew the risks involved; there just weren't any jobs in the States that paid as well for his law enforcement skills. While members of the military were stationed in the country on twelve- to eighteen-month rotations, Buster could come and go with much smaller time commitments. It was one of the reasons why the military didn't always look kindly on contractors who seemed to write their own ticket. Chris Smith was another of the guards protecting Prince on his trip. A Blackwater veteran, he had started with the company on the State Department's Worldwide Personal Protective Services contract in Baghdad three years earlier. With a background in law enforcement and narcotics, the Afghanistan mission seemed the perfect fit for his skills.

Blackwater contractors were paid in the neighborhood of $500 to $600 a day depending on the job, and those who worked in more dangerous environments took home more to show for it.

It was Prince's way of allowing the market to address the problem of getting people to take the tough jobs.

THERE WAS LITTLE DOUBT that the streets of Kabul still posed a danger some six years after the U.S. invasion of Afghanistan. Sadly, the security situation was only getting worse. Prince drove past the Serena Hotel on the way to his next meeting. The hotel was a draw for contractors and international forces alike, as it was the Shangri-La of Afghanistan, a hotel that offered Western-style luxuries. Just weeks after Prince's visit, however, Taliban militants walked into the hotel and unleashed a brutal attack. Using grenades and gunfire, they stormed the halls, leaving behind a trail of dead bodies. One of the attackers even blew himself up. The Taliban were finding it relatively easy to move from regions of Pakistan into Afghanistan to launch attacks, then retreat again. It only amplified the importance of securing the border. As Prince's convoy pulled into the drive of the border police headquarters, he glanced in his notebook. He was meeting with the Afghan general in charge of border patrol operations, and he was running late.

Eight of General Rahman's deputies were already waiting in a large office on the second floor of the two-story building when Prince arrived. He took a seat on a large sofa and listened as the general, through an interpreter, gave him an update on just how Blackwater's training program was working out. Prince's men were responsible not only for training the Afghan force in firearms procedures, but for equipping them as well. It was the "one-stop shopping" that Prince had put into place for his law enforcement and Special Forces clients back at Blackwater's Moyock facility so many years earlier. "Make yourself indispensable to the client," he had said, "and you'll always have work."

A U.S. Army colonel mentoring the border patrol training program sat quietly taking notes in the corner of the room as the general spoke. The son of a prominent former U.S. Republican senator was on Prince's security detail and sat not far from him. He did not want his identity reported. The border had been divided into regions being aided by different members of NATO's International Security Assistance Force (ISAF), yet there were significant problems with militants crossing regularly from Pakistan. Prince had heard that some of the border guards had completed the training and then promptly sold their expensive equipment to willing buyers. Prince told the general that he didn't believe training was enough, and that he really wanted to see a more substantial mentoring program put into place. Prince's men currently served some two weeks with the Afghan units after the Afghans graduated from Blackwater's training program. Prince argued that his men needed to embed with the units for six months or longer to really be effective and to increase the confidence of the Afghans, who would ultimately be left to do their job alone.

DRUGS WERE ANOTHER SERIOUS ISSUE in Afghanistan, and another opportunity for Prince. Months before Prince's trip, the United Nations had estimated that more than 90 percent of the world's opiate supply originated in Afghanistan. While there had been a brief drop in the cultivation of the poppy plant in 2005, production had come back with a vengeance and was generating revenues estimated in the billions of dollars. Much of that money was believed to be funding the Taliban's increased attacks on American and coalition troops, particularly in areas to the south like Helmand Province.

The U.S. government tried both the carrot and the stick, but the carrot was never quite enough. Farmers could find no other crops that yielded the income that poppy did. The stick effort failed as well, as drug eradication efforts seemed to have little actual effect. The farmers continued to grow poppy across several regions, and not surprisingly, the areas where the security threat was the highest were the areas that seemed to produce the most poppy. The situation was so bad that President Hamid Karzai had been quoted as saying, "Once we thought terrorism was Afghanistan's biggest enemy; poppy, its cultivation, and drugs are Afghanistan's major enemy."

Spearheaded by the Department of State, the U.S. government employed a five-pillar approach to tackling Afghanistan's drug problem. The first was a public information campaign aimed at convincing Afghan farmers that despite their livelihood or agricultural traditions, growing poppy plants was a bad thing to do. The second pillar offered incentives for growing other crops. While U.S. officials knew there was no other crop that would offer the same returns, they hoped to use other means to drive up the risks involved with poppy cultivation, namely pillar number three, eradication. It could be dangerous work. Poppy eradication program teams were responsible for monitoring whether locals were complying with the ban on poppy cultivation. It was their job to interact, monitor, and, when necessary, order the eradication of fields found to be in violation of the ban. That call would then be answered by the Afghan Eradication Force. But it wasn't working out as well as the State Department had hoped.

The fourth pillar was interdiction, efforts toward decreasing the trafficking and processing of the poppy into opium. For this, an alliance had been formed between the U.S. Drug Enforcement Administration, the Department of Defense, and the Counter

Narcotics Police of Afghanistan. But if the National Interdiction Unit (NIU) was to be functional, it would need a lot of training in firearms, raid execution, arrest procedures, interviewing suspects, and evidence collection. All of them were items that would be contracted out—many of them to Blackwater.

The fifth pillar, law enforcement and justice reform, was a direct measure to improve the rule of law. Drug detection and eradication weren't enough; the Afghan government needed a structure for arresting, detaining, and trying alleged criminals. The United States ran a central training center higher up along a Kabul mountainside, and that's where Prince was headed next.

Nobody can accuse Blackwater of actively encouraging the drug trade in Afghanistan. Yet, as any economist can recognize, the company's incentives were complicated: as long as the drug trade continued, and as long as the company remained in the good graces of the Afghan and U.S. governments, it would have work. Prince's men had been contracted to help train narcotics officers in the NIU. Intercepting drug shipments was not a job for the faint of heart. Drug traffickers had successfully been transporting poppy out of the country on the backs of donkeys traveling narrow mountainous passes along the border. Other drug runners had loaded the drug into the back of pickup trucks, often taking little effort to cover it up. Those shipments had been fairly easily detected, but stopping a drug shipment one truck at a time wasn't going to stop the flow of narcotics out of the country. Afghans had to be trained in more aggressive tactics, such as how to conduct a successful raid, how to collect and interpret intelligence, and how to fight their way out of an ambush. Many parts of Afghanistan were still under the influence of powerful drug lords who ruled their territory with an iron fist.

Being a part of the Pentagon's Narcoterrorism Technology

program would also be profitable. Five companies stood to support the program, worth up to $15 billion. Blackwater had a K-9 unit back at Moyock that trained dogs in explosives and drug detection, and Prince knew the dogs could do the same work in Afghanistan. He would soon send over a dog and a handler to prove his point.

PRINCE BOUNDED OUT of the SUV and into the NIU's new training facility. While the flat concrete buildings may have seemed underwhelming to a Westerner, in Afghanistan, they were state-of-the-art. The training facility had classrooms and outside instruction ranges, as well as a cafeteria for feeding the trainees. Prince ate lunch with the director of the facility and headed outside to watch some of the training already in progress. He noticed small details: how the Afghan students held their weapons with their fingers off the triggers, how they approached their targets. In the classrooms he talked briefly with the instructors about the challenges of working through interpreters and again was asked to pose for pictures with some of his men who had only heard stories about him but had never met the man himself.

Just up the hill, a new shooting range was under construction by the Army Corps of Engineers. When completed, it would be the most advanced, high-tech range in Afghanistan, and according to those in the know, it rivaled any of the top ten shooting ranges in the United States.

As students finished up shooting practice on a different nearby range, they came to say hello to Prince. They had been practicing with guns mounted in the back of pickup trucks, shooting against targets tucked into the hillside. They only had to ask Prince once if he wanted to give it a try. He climbed into the back of one of the small trucks and laid his hands on the weapon. He sized up the target and pressed his finger on the trigger. Any day he could fire a weapon on a training course was a good day for Prince.

After about twenty minutes, C.T. ushered the group back into the waiting vehicles and briefed the boss on the remaining itinerary on the way back to the safe house. A vendor would be meeting Prince at the house, and after that, Prince would address a meeting of his men, followed by a quick trip down the street to that "other government agency."

Despite a busy day and lingering jet lag, Prince met over dinner with a local vendor who was having trouble getting logistical support equipment where it needed to be. As the two talked, some thirty Blackwater men gathered in the next room, waiting to meet Prince. They knew that the company had taken a PR beating and wondered what Prince would have to say to them. Prince finished up a plate of food and told the vendor he'd have to finish the conversation later. Prince headed into the next room to address his men.

"Times have been tough," he began, "but you guys have been doing great work, and I need you to keep doing it." The front room of the house where Prince was staying was crowded. Some of the men stood awkwardly in doorways just to get a better view. Prince was candid about what the company had gone through since the shooting in Nisoor Square just two months earlier, reminding them that one crucial mistake wipes out a whole lot of "atta boys." It had become one of his favorite phrases. Prince reminded the men that the work they were doing was important, but that it was also important to make good decisions. He finally stopped to ask if they had any questions; there was only one. One of the men wanted to know about the future of the company, and whether they would still have jobs a year from now. Prince

assured him that the company was still doing well, despite calls
from some on the Hill to have it banned, and that he planned
to be around for a very long time. It was a boilerplate response;
in fact, he had already wondered aloud to those close to him
whether the political price was worth it. He almost seemed to
debate retiring or selling the company off.

Yet it was hard to imagine Prince doing anything else. His
restless energy, ADD-like attention span, and unwavering self-
confidence, combined with the rapidly expanding commitments
of the U.S. military, made it just too tempting for him to not
continue to build his empire.

THE KABUL SKY was dark and gray as Prince's convoy made its
way to the U.S. embassy not far from the Blackwater safe houses.
Maneuvering through the maze of concrete barriers and barbed
wire, C.T. briefed the boss on what was coming next. He had
arranged another briefing on the border control situation, specifically the Afghan border police, this one at the U.S. embassy.

In a dark office in the basement of the embassy building
with fluorescent lights flickering, Prince sat down to be briefed
on what he largely already knew. In a PowerPoint presentation,
another contractor flashed a colorful map of Afghanistan on the
pulled-down screen, highlighting the border regions in colorful
lines. A blue arrow pointed to the area where Prince's own men
were to begin two-week mentorship programs with the Afghans
they had trained. Prince still thought that needed to be longer.
He was also told that not all of the ISAF countries in charge of
different parts of the border were fully coordinating their plans
for border security. After about forty-five minutes, Prince left
the briefing, chuckling about the irony of a contractor brief-

ing a contractor about the largely contracted efforts along the border.

There would be some good news for Prince out of this trip: the Army liked his mentor proposal. Prince would be back a couple more times in the following year, once going out into the field with a team himself to try to convince the Army that Blackwater was the company to head up the mentor effort as they looked to expand the program. The Pentagon would eventually decide that they wanted Blackwater to take over a larger portion of the border patrol training. The Canadians were also talking seriously about a national dog program and were looking to bring in some eighty trained dogs and handlers to sniff out drugs in Afghanistan. The Canadians were considering putting some $4.5 million into the effort. Blackwater wanted the contract. Because of the political sensitivities surrounding the company, C.T. wondered whether they would have to run the business through Greystone International. The name wasn't nearly as radioactive as Blackwater had become.

IT WAS EARLY in the morning when Prince piled into the waiting SUV for another trip to the Kabul airport. This time, he was headed out to Forward Operating Base Salerno, one of the remote frontiers of the military, and one of its largest. Camp Salerno sits in Khowst Province, near the Pakistani border. It appears to sit in the middle of nowhere, but by many estimates, there are hundreds of Taliban and al-Qaeda militants that call the area home, and the base had come under attack numerous times by small bands of militants. Prince's men were on a far less controversial mission here than those in Baghdad were, though not without its own risks. They were supporting the Department of Defense by providing aircraft and pilots to fly "bundle drop" missions to soldiers operating even farther afield, with even less security. The "bundles" were metal crates packed with essential supplies—food, weapons, even U.S. mail—and were harnessed to parachutes before being loaded into the back of Prince's CASAs for several flights per week.

Prince took a moment to talk with the American soldiers on the ground before joining them for a mission brief. Standing on the landing strip, he listened as the men and women were told how important it was to make sure their harnesses were secured inside the back of the plane, and how to push each bundle out the open back. There was also a sobering reminder that these missions were being flown in hostile territory. Planes had come under small arms fire from the ground in the past. Evasive maneuvers would be necessary. The pilots would fly fast and low, so this wasn't a mission for anyone prone to motion sickness.

Prince took off his suit jacket and pulled the canvas harness straps up through his legs before climbing into the back of the aircraft and attaching the metal buckle to a ring attached to the plane. Given all the political problems his company was facing at home, these were the moments he loved. As the plane took off, Prince gazed out the open hole in the back. It had snowed overnight in the mountains, and the narrow peaks began to close in around the plane as the pilots maneuvered their way into a narrow valley pass. It was clear to see why small arms attacks from the ground could be dangerous, as the plane hugged the landscape. Soon, the order came from the cockpit to move into position, and the men and women in uniform joined Prince in pushing the bundle into place. Moments later, the signal came, and the bundle was shoved from the plane. As the parachute deployed and the package drifted down to its target, motion sickness threatened everyone on board. The soldiers sat down, looking out the window and trying to concentrate on the fresh air coming at them. Prince went along for several more drops before finally calling it a day, shaking hands, and posing for more pictures.

(Several months after Prince's visit to Salerno, the base came under coordinated attack by six men wearing suicide vests. The men had planned to blow an entry point into the base for another group of attackers to follow. Their mission failed when three of the suicide bombers were shot and the remaining devices detonated prematurely. Just two days before that, suicide bombers detonated explosives packed into vehicles near the camp's entrance. There was a dangerous decline in security on both sides of the border that would only make those missions harder.)

AS THE LONG WEEK wound to an end, Prince prepared for what was waiting for him at home. The Nisoor Square shooting had not come up much for him here, though he admitted privately that potential clients had worried about associating with Blackwater. While they liked Prince and the services he provided, they faced political pressure based on the company's reputation. Prince knew the company had become radioactive. Near the Kabul airport, Prince stopped at a PX, one of the stores that serve armed forces around the world. He walked the aisles stocked with everything from iPods to corn chips, until he reached the section selling Blackwater gear. Blackwater underwear was selling for $12 a pair. Back home in Moyock, the Blackwater tactical shop had expanded as well. People just couldn't buy enough of their T-shirts. Political trouble notwithstanding, Blackwater was no longer just a name, it was a brand. The Blackwater bear paw wasn't yet as recognizable as the Nike swoosh, but it was gaining ground.

THE VIP WAITING ROOM at the Kabul airport wouldn't have been bad if Prince had spent less time there. As a twenty-minute delay turned into an hour delay for Prince's flight back to Dubai, the blaring music from the television in the corner began to take its toll. Prince hopped to his feet and headed toward C.T. "There's got to be another plane to Dubai, and we've got to get on it," he said tersely. When Prince got impatient, the blood pressure of everyone around him ticked up significantly. He admitted that he was not a patient man. He was not convinced that patience was, in fact, a virtue. His mood could turn from bad to worse at the drop of a hat, depending largely on whether he felt someone was wasting his time. He grabbed C.T. and circled back around to the main entrance of the airport, where the security guards insisted on patting him down thoroughly. He made his way through a baggage check area to the sales desk of another airline. "I need four tickets to Dubai," he said. "How soon can you get me there?" As the man behind the desk tapped quickly on his keyboard, Prince reached for his credit card. The boarding passes were just about printed when Prince got a call from C.T. that the other airplane was starting to board.

CHAPTER 11

The Blackwater Behemoth

ON A WALL in Gary Jackson's office just near the door hung a poster that summed up how far the company had come. He liked to call it his "actual, not virtual" poster. Against a backdrop of sea, land, and air, it showed an artist's depiction of the assets Blackwater had been able either to build or to acquire in its first ten years: an unmanned airship; a Super Tucano jet; a CASA aircraft much like those the company used on contract for the Department of Defense in Afghanistan; a Puma armored vehicle; a 183-foot maritime vessel dubbed the *McArthur*; some smaller boats; and an armored personnel carrier that Blackwater manufactured and dubbed "The Grizzly."

"Virtual, virtual, virtual," said Jackson as he showed off the poster. "All the big defense companies can do is virtual this or virtual that. We actually do it. It's not a virtual world; it's about getting it done." The contrast of Blackwater's equipment and power with its humble beginnings is evident in another poster hanging on Jackson's wall. An artist's rendering of the original

Blackwater concept in Moyock: a central lodge, surrounded by a number of shooting ranges, with just a handful of other buildings. Moyock had four times as many buildings, and Blackwater has other facilities around the world.

Jackson's ability to get things done is exactly the reason Prince had remained steadfastly loyal to the fellow former Navy SEAL. There had been numerous occasions over the years when others had counseled Prince that Jackson was the wrong man for the job, that he didn't have the kind of strategic development experience that Blackwater needed. Yet Prince's loyalties remained with the man he trusted the most. The relationship between the two had several parts: Jackson was part business partner, part counselor, and part trusted confidant concerning the difficulties Prince had faced in his private life. The two have been together for nearly a dozen years, through the loss of Prince's first wife and through Prince's affair with the couple's former nanny.

In turn, Jackson, a recovering alcoholic, felt an unmatched loyalty to Prince. Working for Blackwater had changed Jackson's life in many ways. After living for years on a military salary, Jackson was able to enjoy the spoils of success. A self-described car fanatic, Jackson had purchased at least five cars, including a Porsche, an old truck that he was restoring, and a 1953 Jaguar.

People who have worked with the two describe them as an old married couple, something they both take in stride. "I think both of our wives would say that," joked Jackson.

Prince insisted that in some ways, their relationship is better than a marriage. "We've never thrown furniture," said Prince. "We've never gotten close to blows, never even once. So in that sense, it's far more fortunate than in a marriage. We have never been mad enough to say something insulting."

It was normal for the two to be on the phone together multiple times a day. When they fought, they usually did it behind the closed door of Jackson's office. The relationship worked, in part, because Prince spent much of his time up in McLean, while Jackson ran the show in Moyock.

The two men have a lot in common: former military experience, a passion to get things done, and the patience of a gnat with attention deficit disorder.

"We make decisions fast. Fight, and clash, resolution, and move on," said Prince. "If you're on a sea patrol and you're pissed about some decision the lieutenant made, the mission continues, get on with it."

Much like in a military chain of command, Prince and Jackson knew their places. There was no board of directors at Blackwater; the chain of command was tight, and Jackson had his ways of getting the boss to do what he wanted by either stalling long enough until the situation changed, or commissioning others to lobby for a change of course. Their intense relationship defined the company in many ways.

"We don't run this place like a normal company," noted Prince.

Nearly a dozen vice presidents at Blackwater helped oversee the tremendous expansion the company had enjoyed in the past few years. All of them reported to Jackson. Former employees say that crossing him is usually a career-ender. It doesn't help that the company was full of alpha-male personalities. It is one of the things that led Jackson to incorporate the "fifteen-minute pissed off" rule: employees were allowed to be angry about something for fifteen minutes, then they needed to get on with the business at hand.

While some saw Jackson as a visionary, others saw him as little more than an operator who won Prince's loyalties by keeping his secrets. But that charge misses a crucial trait that defines Jackson for Prince: Jackson is a doer.

"I acknowledge that a dollar and a vision will buy you a cup of coffee," said Prince. "Gary executes; he makes the stuff happen."

If there was a constant at Blackwater, it was change. The company that began as little more than a training facility had grown in ways that the original founders, many of whom are no longer there, couldn't have imagined. There had been tremendous growing pains along the way. In the beginning, Prince grabbed all the local talent he could get as needs arose. The company's revenues quickly began to explode.

"This business was growing so fast," said Jackson. "Every three months it was a different business." Both Jackson and Prince soon realized that if Blackwater was to compete with Fortune 500 companies, it needed Fortune 500 experience. It was fine that they had hired a lot of local talent, but as the company grew, Prince and Jackson let a lot of those loyal employees go. It was something that Prince believed needed to be done.

"I think with some people," said Prince, "we left them in certain positions longer than they should have been."

As company executives came and went, several of them believed that the relationship between the two men was a big part of the problems the company faced. Several cited instances where Prince simply refused to consider that his number two was doing anything wrong. Some thought that Prince protected Jackson at the expense of better judgment, an accusation that irritated the CEO.

"I don't protect Gary," said Prince. "Gary does a great job. Every day he wakes up running, and this place is not a democracy. We take input from all kinds of people all the time, but ultimately somebody's gotta make a decision."

In January 2007, as Prince huddled with leaders in the Pentagon to discuss the new rules following the September 16 incident, the *Harvard Business Review* published an article entitled "Moments of Truth." It was a series of candid essays by global executives about the challenges they had faced that had helped shape them as leaders. Gary Jackson was profiled, along with executives from Coca-Cola, Ernst & Young, and Nokia.

Jackson argued in the article that the corporate culture at Blackwater was the secret behind the company's success. Blackwater was run much like a military unit, but with a firm focus on the bottom line. Jackson was so intent on surrounding himself with others like him that he had compiled a database of job candidates that he marked with either a *T* or a *D* to differentiate between a "talker" and a "doer."

Jackson told the *HBR* editors, "I constantly push for the 80 percent solution that is executable now over the 100 percent solution we might be able to devise in another three weeks."

But the culture that Jackson was so proud of was also the culture that drew the most fire from critics. A former company executive complained that corners had been cut in the interest of all those 80 percent solutions. It was the claim argued by the victims' families in the case against the company over the Fallujah atrocity. According to former employees, one of Blackwater's own executives, in an internal report, detailed corners that were cut in that instance: the company had too few men in the convoys, for starters. The former executive believed that, as a result, lives were put at risk. He traced what he called a path of stupid decisions back to Gary Jackson. Another employee who said he had seen the report characterized it as a damning detailed account of the company's missteps. Jackson and Prince saw things differently and insisted lessons were learned from that horrific day.

"Anytime you have guys that are killed, you always look back and see how you try to avoid that next time," said Prince. "But it is a war zone and you have insurgents, terrorists that are actively plotting to kill your guys."

Changes were made after Fallujah based in part on the internal review. But Jackson, without admitting wrongdoing in the Fallujah case, insisted that change was part of the normal routine at Blackwater.

"Change has been made since 1998," said Jackson. "I make mistakes every day. The goal for everybody here is you can make mistakes, we're not gonna pull your toenails out if you make a mistake, but don't make the mistake again."

While Jackson and Prince both admitted that a lack of patience was their biggest problem, they also insisted that its flip side, flexibility, was the reason for the company's astounding growth. Blackwater had been named by *Fast Company* magazine as one of the fastest-growing companies in the United States, putting Gary Jackson's name right up there with Bill Gates. The article touted Jackson's "private army" as being essential to the continuing effort in Iraq. The article also named Bill Clinton for his foundation work. The magazine editors invited those who made the list to a party at Studio One in New York. Jackson, Prince, and then–company vice president Chris Taylor made the trip. The men made an awkward attempt to blend in.

"I walked in and looked at the editor and said, 'Do you know who we are?' I was like, 'Are you sure you understand?'" recalled Jackson.

Prince and Jackson led by example, even to the point of maintaining a physical training regimen much like the physical training requirements in the military. The PT program is "strongly encouraged" among Blackwater employees.

"If he and I and most of this second floor [the executive office holders] are out there dragging tires down the road and people are in their [offices], if they are sitting at their desks, they are hiding their faces," said Jackson. "They're not stuffing stuff into their face."

The company had a corporate Weight Watchers program and two gymnasiums built for employees who shared Jackson's zeal for staying in top physical condition. Also keeping with a tradition more likely found in the military than in corporate America, Blackwater employed both a corporate master chief petty officer and a full-time chaplain. Critics argued lots of reasons why a business cannot be run like the military, but none of them mattered at Blackwater. Prince was sure that his company was more efficient than almost any other government agency, as well as many of his competitors. But Blackwater was a company thriving off the American taxpayer, more so than most other private companies.

Jackson and Prince both liked pointing out that Blackwater was lean by most standards, and they even compared it to their biggest client, the State Department's Diplomatic Security Service. "The Diplomatic Security Service: 35,000 people, 1,500 operators," said Jackson.

"We field that many operators with how many people assigned to our program?" asked Prince. "Fifty?"

"Fifteen," Jackson responded. "OK, let's go big, a hundred people, which no way, but that would be all the overhead, everything, one hundred people, and we're running in rotation, about 6,000 people a year; yeah, they've got 35,000."

"You can quote me on this," said Prince. "The next time there's a snow emergency in Washington, and they say all nonessential personnel can stay home, they should stay home for good."

"You wanna reduce the size of government?" asked Prince with a snap of his fingers. "Simple."

They love to disparage what they call a behemoth government, yet their clients are almost all government agencies. "We didn't grow this business because of politics, or contacts, or somebody in the White House saying, 'Hey, give Blackwater the job,'" Prince insisted. "We have grown the business by doing what our customers need us to do, period. We run hard and get the damn job done."

Yet in truth, Blackwater won a lot of contracts by default: they were the only contractor big enough and well equipped enough to take on many jobs for the U.S. government. And most of Blackwater's employees are former military men—that is, government types.

"A lot of guys who come here are operators, and they are used to asking for more budgets," said Prince. "When the money runs out, they ask for more budget. We can't do that; there's no guarantee that Blackwater will exist if we don't look at the bottom line. We have to make enough money to be able to keep the lights on, to reinvest, to continue to execute. If you're not making money, it's not a business, it's charity."

JACKSON'S CORNER OFFICE overlooked the headquarters of the Blackwater empire. The company had its roots in the training business and had expanded in the past decade to include two other training centers outside of the main 7,000-acre facility in Moyock.

Blackwater North, in Mt. Carroll, Illinois, was run much like a smaller version of the Moyock facility. It was a place where Joe Public can walk in for a class on basic shooting or driving. Blackwater North focused on courses for military and law enforcement, from basic sniper skills to extreme officer survival courses to hostage rescue scenarios. It also offered specialty courses in executive protection. A five-day class included instruction in motorcade procedures and threat scenarios. The cost was $1,300. Lunch was free.

The company had also opened a training facility in San Diego known as Blackwater West, but not without a fight. Blackwater's original plans were to open a facility that would cater to the U.S. Navy by offering a place where sailors could train on multiple firing ranges as well as in the classroom and simulated settings. But plans to build the facility on a Southern California chicken and cattle ranch were met with ferocious opposition. The company eventually opened a 61,000-square-foot training facility in an industrial building near the U.S.–Mexico border, but it took a federal judge to declare that the training could begin, defeating attempts by local leaders to withhold permits and opposition from Congressman Bob Filner, who worried that the company was trying to get a foothold near the border, where it could then offer private migrant or drug interdiction services, much like what it was doing in Afghanistan.

Blackwater used the facility—equipped with an indoor firing range and mock ships—to train U.S. sailors in counterterrorism techniques as part of a $400 million contract from the U.S. Navy that grew out of the original contract the company had after the bombing of the USS *Cole*. The West Coast facility catered to sailors stationed at Pacific bases. Blackwater had trained more than one hundred thousand students and continued to host about five hundred more each day, teaching everything from shooting to driving to tactical skills.

Just a short way down the road from the new administration building were three separate driving tracks offering students experience on all types of surfaces. It was a training ground meant to prepare them for defensive driving under hostile conditions. There was also a complex Prince refered to as "Little Baghdad," a series of small buildings where security forces tested their skills at urban warfare. Jackson also built a mock train and R U Ready High School—prompted by the Columbine shootings—so that law enforcement officers could run hostage simulations.

Blackwater K-9 was based in Moyock, offering trained dogs for use by law enforcement, the military, and commercial businesses. Prince also purchased a video production company for cranking out a line of instructional DVDs aimed at law enforcement. The productions focused on everything from lifesaving medical techniques to emergency response measures.

In addition to the several shooting ranges, Blackwater had an armory stacked high with row upon row of firearms. Some were kept in a locked vault. The company had not only acquired weapons for local law enforcement, it had also designed its own rifle, the BW-15, which it fully customized for clients. Prince even gave one to Jackson as a Christmas present.

Blackwater had its share of troubles with the guns kept on the property. The ATF raided the facility in June 2008 as part of an investigation into whether Blackwater had tried to get around federal laws that prohibited the private purchase of automatic assault rifles. Federal agents confiscated almost two dozen automatic weapons, including AK-47s. The company explained that the guns were owned by the Camden County sheriff's department and that Blackwater stored them at the sheriff's request.

PERHAPS THE MOST IMPRESSIVE ASSET at Moyock was the vehicles depicted in the poster hanging in Jackson's office. In the expansion of the past several years, Prince had invested heavily in research, development, and acquisition. It was the one thing that set him apart from most of his competitors; he had the money to bankroll multimillion-dollar projects on his own.

The company had purchased light infantry fighting vehicles known as Pumas and shipped them to Iraq. With a three- to six-person crew capability, the Puma was similar to the Bradley fighting vehicle.

Early in 2007, Defense Secretary Robert Gates made clear that the U.S. military needed more Mine Resistant Ambush Protected (MRAP) vehicles, and it needed them now, suggesting that scores of Americans might die every month that MRAP deliveries were delayed. While not fail-safe, the MRAP armored vehicles were the best chance U.S. troops had for defeating the effectiveness of improvised explosive devices being used against them by insurgents in Iraq.

Prince wanted in on the deal and had already begun research and development on his own mine-resistant vehicle called "The Grizzly." The bulky, beasty vehicle incorporated a patented armor protection system that withstood an IED blast in initial testing. Prince sunk tens of millions into the project and even established an assembly line right on the Moyock property. He had hoped to lease the vehicles to the U.S. military, but things didn't quite work out that way. The military declined the offer. A dozen Grizzlies sat outside the Blackwater building where they were manufactured. Vice President Bill Mathews touts the fact that the vehicle performed so well in the testing rounds.

"The great thing is that we had the opportunity to go through the testing process," said Mathews. "The credibility alone was worth it." But former employees who believe Prince had sunk upwards of $25 million into the project shook their heads in disbelief at the waste.

Prince called the experience "painful," saying that the bidding process within the Pentagon was a "closed-door society, wrapped in politics and the retired generals' network." It was a frustrated response to the fact that his vehicle simply hadn't drawn enough attention in the crowded defense contractor market.

Prince had made other investments that had yet to pay off. One was a 183-foot maritime vessel dubbed the *McArthur*. The ship, complete with a satellite-based communications system and helicopter landing pad, was originally intended to serve as a training platform for the military and law enforcement in conducting peacekeeping operations.

Blackwater would later market the vessel as an escort for private companies battling piracy in the waters of the Gulf of Aden. While the company would need a State Department license to operate such missions, Prince wasn't outwardly concerned about finding clients. He envisioned a "pay as you go" scenario, where he would charge companies safe-passage fees by the trip.

And then there was the airship. Blackwater had built a remotely piloted airship vehicle with the capacity to fly unmanned. Once again, the ship was built without a buyer. Prince was convinced the vehicle would prove itself as a useful tool for monitoring border areas, or areas where twenty-four-hour surveillance was needed. The company advertised the ship on its Web site, saying that it will begin selling or leasing airships to the Department of Defense, Department of Homeland Security, and other federal, state, and local government customers. The ship had captured the attention of the Navy for its ability to provide unmanned surveillance for up to seventy-two hours at a time. But so far, there were no contracts for it. It was another multimillion-dollar investment on spec.

Prince hadn't just built his own craft, he had also acquired high-profile tools for the Blackwater arsenal. One of them was a Super Tucano aircraft, built by Brazilian jet maker Embraer for the Brazilian air force; the company developed a variant of the plane known as an ALX, or light attack aircraft. One of the things Prince liked about it was that the Tucano could fly day or night and could land on remote, unpaved runways. It needed very little ground support. Used for training, the Tucano was also marketed for border patrol and counterinsurgency operations, areas where Prince very much wanted to expand the business. While company executives touted the plane for training and demonstration, they had set their sights on leasing it, along with a pilot, for counterinsurgency operations. Was the world ready for a contractor in the pilot's seat of a military jet, with his finger on the trigger? Though he wouldn't give specifics, Prince was considering leasing the Tucano out on an hourly basis to a U.S. government agency in what he hoped would turn into a highly valuable, and highly classified, contract.

BEFORE THE FALLOUT FROM THE NISOOR SQUARE SHOOTING, security was still a massive part of the Blackwater revenue stream, accounting for at least 50 percent of the company's business. Some estimates put it closer to 80 percent. Blackwater had a database of some forty thousand operators available at a moment's notice, most with either military or law enforcement experience. The company kept gear ready to fly off the shelves for last-minute deployments, and Blackwater maintained a steady flow of contractors. Jackson argued that moving away from that part of the business wouldn't be a game ender.

Blackwater had security contracts in only two countries, but they were big ones. "All the rest we do aviation training, we do the infrastructure, building, so there's only two security contracts left that we're a part of [the State Department and the CIA], that we'd really want to be a part of, and we already have the market share on both of them."

At the same time, Prince ran several security contracts through his other companies, like Greystone, in part to avoid any connection to the Blackwater name. Vice President Chris Burgess oversaw the company's foreign entities, not just Greystone, but also Salamis, Prince's aviation holding company, and al Zalama, Iraq's version of an employment agency.

Burgess saw stark differences in how Blackwater was perceived outside the United States.

"There are two perspectives overseas," said Burgess. "What is generally being said on Al Jazeera: that Blackwater is the evil company, the wing of the U.S. government, cowboys running rampant; whereas you talk to the leaders of the country [Jordan, United Arab Emirates], and they say, 'Hey, can you guys provide us some training?'"

But there was growing concern among company executives that the reputation could start overshadowing the quality of the work. "As somebody once told Bill, 'We're in the big leagues now,' and people are going to try to knock us off our pedestal, and we're in a very dangerous business," said Burgess. "If it just keeps getting worse and worse, the Blackwater name could get so tainted and diluted, I hate to say deadly. Radioactive: I mean, that's definitely a possibility, and that's a concern, I think, with all of us."

Prince was convinced that aviation offered the way ahead. Blackwater had built a small airport on its North Carolina land, with a 6,000-foot-long runway, a smaller 2,550-foot airstrip, and a 20,000-square-foot aircraft hangar.

Presidential Airways had experienced enormous success contracting out its fleet of CASA 212 light transport planes that the
military was using in Afghanistan. Prince liked to talk publicly
about how his men had flown eleven thousand sorties in Afghanistan in 2007 supporting some thirty-eight combat posts.

Prince estimated he'd lost some $10 million worth of aviation
equipment in Iraq and Afghanistan, all of it self-insured (that is,
uninsured). Yet he believed the business was still a moneymaker.
The State Department leased several helicopters retrofitted with
war zone equipment, and Presidential Airways was still flying
high for the Department of Defense in Afghanistan, with more
than $100 million in contracts in the country.

Finally, training remained high on the agenda. Blackwater had
secured quite a few high-profile training contracts, among them
training the security detail for leaders like King Abdullah II of
Jordan and training Greek police for security before the 2004
Summer Olympics. They had even been contacted by Pakistani
presidential hopeful Benazir Bhutto to help provide security for
her during a turbulent election, but Prince says problems with the
paperwork at the State Department held up the process. Bhutto
was assassinated after a political rally in Rawalpindi, Pakistan, in
December 2007. Prince says Blackwater was also approached to
provide training for Chinese security prior to the 2008 Olympics,
but that he turned them down, worried that the training could
later be used against Americans in some way.

WITH MORE THAN a dozen federal agencies having launched
investigations into the company, Prince had moments when he
wondered about the future. Sometimes, he contemplated a total
change. He is wealthy. He didn't need to take the grief caused by

Blackwater's radioactivity. He could afford to do something else. Yet his personality is relentless—he's a fighter; it's hard to imagine him just walking away from his empire.

Financially, Prince had enough of costly investments in research and development that failed to pay off. He was looking for a silent partner to inject cash into the operation. Blackwater had entered talks months earlier with the equity fund Cerebus Capital Management, but Cerebus broke off negotiations after the talks were leaked to a news network. So Prince continued to search.

Prince spoke openly of expecting revenues of $1 billion a year by 2010. Still, Jackson was confident that there was no other company out there like his. He simply did not think the State Department had any other options.

"Lots and lots of people are going to build a Blackwater facility," said Jackson. "If they start right now, they might get it done; if they have $100 million that they could just toss at it, they might get it done in five to seven years."

Prince knew that for his company to survive, it would have to stay lean and hungry.

"The lion wakes up in the morning; he knows he has to outrun the gazelle, or he's gonna starve," said Prince. "The gazelle wakes up and knows he has to outrun the lion, or he's gonna be eaten. The moral of the story is, whether you're the lion or the gazelle, when you wake up, you'd better be running."

CHAPTER 12

The Cost of Business

THE NISOOR SQUARE SHOOTING had a huge impact on the way the U.S. government employed its contractors in Iraq. Months after the shooting, the Pentagon's man on the subject, Jack Bell, spoke with the Iraqi minister of defense to try to gauge just how hot the temperature still was on the subject. "He was very articulate and very concerned, but he said that it is absolutely the intention of the Iraqi government that they get control of what he called the 'Blackwaters'—meaning the State Department security agents—and that that event never be allowed to happen again."

The temperature was gauged back in Moyock as well. The Canadian police had canceled a training program with Total Intel, citing Nisoor Square. Prince's relationship with the Pentagon remained in place—by mid-January 2008, the DoD had renewed his Presidential Airways contract for heavy-lift fixed-wing aircraft, personnel, and equipment, worth just under $51 million, and additional contracts trickled in over the coming months. Yet the impact of the shooting was felt inside the corridors of the Pentagon. Blackwater continued to be paid, but the company was now intensely disliked by people at the highest levels.

At the end of January 2008, the U.S. State Department team, headed by Ambassador John Negroponte, and the Department of Defense team, headed by Deputy Secretary of Defense Gordon England, called all Iraq security contractors to a closed-door meeting for a reading of the new rules that would govern their actions in Iraq. Deputy Under Secretary of Defense Jack Bell and Ambassador Pat Kennedy presented the findings of their investigations to some twenty company representatives who showed up for the three-hour session. The unwitting guest of honor was Erik Prince. It was the first time that Bell or Kennedy had met the young CEO. They shook his hand and exchanged pleasantries, but not everyone in the room was happy to see him.

"Quite frankly, the whole reason why we had to have that meeting was because of him and his organization," said another DoD official.

The Departments of Defense and State had worked together on a Memorandum of Agreement, a set of guidelines for how the two departments would better coordinate the movement and oversight of their contractors in Iraq. Defense Secretary Gates had initially entertained the idea that all contractors in the country should fall under his military control. State had resisted. In the end, it was mutually agreed that there had to be far better communication between the State Department contractors and the military. The final authority for the movements of contractors through specific areas lay with the chief of mission, Ambassador Ryan Crocker.

The agreement also covered the use of force. Shooters were asked to take only well-aimed shots and to consider the safety of innocent civilians. They would also be required to report all shooting incidents immediately. It wasn't much of a change, essentially just a request to "please be careful." The real issue remained: when contractors broke the rules, who would punish them?

PRINCE FACED A GREATER WORRY than this meeting and its minor adjustments to the rules. Had Blackwater and all it touched become so radioactive that the State Department might cancel the company's biggest contract? Prince had hoped by now to have published his own book about Blackwater, touting all the reasons why the government needed him, and all of the good work his company had done. According to one insider who had seen parts of the manuscript, it was pure Prince: a rant, showing no mercy toward the company's critics. If Prince couldn't win with the mainstream media, he hoped to have his say in the book. "Whenever it comes up, State gets postal on us," said Prince.

In January 2008, as the FBI investigation into the events of Nisoor Square continued, news surfaced that the main evidence that Prince had cited in defense of his men was covered up, literally.

Holes in the vehicles involved in the shooting were repaired, along with a damaged radiator. Investigators hadn't even gotten a look at them yet. Blackwater said the repairs were made at the direction of the State Department. The State Department wouldn't comment. But regardless of who gave the order, the repairs made it harder for investigators to determine whether the men had actually come under fire, as Prince said they did. The FBI sent teams to Iraq to investigate the shooting, but it would take more than a year from the date of the incident before anything would be known. Prosecutors had already begun calling witnesses before a grand jury.

The families of some of the victims of Nisoor Square had also filed suit in a U.S. court against Blackwater for damages in October 2007. Some of the surviving victims, along with family members of those who perished, claimed that the company operated under "a culture of lawlessness." The suit also claimed that some Blackwater guards used steroids and other "judgment-altering substances." It was something Prince fiercely denied, saying that Blackwater contractors were subject to drug testing as part of the terms of their employment. The suit attempted to put some sort of legal definition to the word-of-mouth reputation the company had gained in Iraq and even within the halls of the Pentagon. The suit called Blackwater's use of force "excessive" and blamed it on company culture. The suit also accused the company of war crimes, wrongful death, and assault, all accusations Blackwater denied.

The new litigants took heart from developments in the older case over the Afghan plane crash. The National Transportation Safety Board found that in that case, Presidential Airways had not provided sufficient oversight and guidance of the pilots involved in the accident. It also said the military didn't provide adequate oversight of the contractors, something that Prince insisted was part of the government's responsibility. It seemed more and more possible that a civil court judge would award damages to the widows. Prince's lawyers had tried to convince a judge that the lawsuit should be dismissed on the grounds that soldiers cannot sue the government, and his men were working as agents of the government. The judge refused. The company had also asked the Bush administration to provide information that might help them make their legal argument, but the court deadline came and went without a word of support from the White House.

Prince was upset. If the State Department had failed to step up after the September shooting incident, then this was the government's chance to come out in strong support of Blackwater—but nobody stepped up for the company. Prince's legal team introduced a new, and somewhat unexpected, argument. The crash had occurred in Afghanistan, a country ruled by Sharia law. Sharia was a combination of Muslim law and religious code based on the teachings of the Qur'an and the customs of the Prophet Muhammad. If the judge agreed that the case fell under the jurisdiction of Sharia law, it would mean the end of the lawsuit, as under Sharia law, a company is not responsible for the actions of its employees.

Prince made the move despite his own distaste for Sharia law. Ironically, his views were playing out on the big screen. Prince had quietly bankrolled a new film, *The Stoning of Soraya M.* It premiered at the Toronto International Film Festival in the fall of 2008. The movie told the tragic story of an Iranian woman whose husband wanted out of the marriage—at any cost. Based on the book by Friedounce Sahebjam, the story graphically detailed Soraya's eventual stoning by a group that included her father and two of her sons. For Prince, it was a public jab at fundamentalist Islam.

NEWS ON THE VARIOUS SUITS came as the company received a one-year reprieve from its biggest financial worry. On Friday, April 4, 2008, Erik Prince was summoned to the State Department's Diplomatic Security headquarters in Roslyn, Virginia. It was still a month before Blackwater's contract for the State Department

would come up for official renewal, and Prince wasn't sure what
to expect. All he knew for sure was that Acting Assistant Secretary of State for Diplomatic Security Greg Starr wanted to talk
to him.

Prince was escorted to Starr's office in the corner of the
building. Surrounded on two sides by walls of windows, he had a
bird's-eye view of the treetops that stretched over D.C. and parts
of Virginia. The meeting was cordial, and the news was good:
Starr informed Prince that the State Department would renew
the contract for another year. But Starr wanted to be sure that
Prince understood who was in charge. The State Department
wanted to handle the press on this one.

"We told him that we were going to pick up the option for another year," said Starr. "I think I made it pretty clear that it was in
our interest that this be announced by the State Department."

It didn't quite happen that way. By early evening, the television
networks had the news. Someone had leaked it. Prince insists
it wasn't him. The State Department started receiving calls for
comment from reporters. Starr explained that the department's
security needs required the renewal. Ambassador Pat Kennedy
went further, saying that the State Department simply couldn't
meet its operational needs in Iraq without Blackwater. The Department of State of the United States of America couldn't do its
job in Iraq without Prince's company.

The news was met with shock, anger, and frustration by Democrats on the Hill. Within a month, Senator John Kerry, then
chair of the Senate Foreign Relations Committee's Middle East
subcommittee, called for hearings into the renewal.

"To learn that Blackwater's no-bid security for Iraq was renewed even as a grand jury investigates the company and the
IRS considers its own review of the company's books, raises seri-

ous concerns that merit Senate hearings. How was this decision made?" asked Kerry in a statement. "What was the process that concluded there were no alternatives?"

In May 2008, some answers were delivered as to just how extensively the U.S. government had come to rely on private contractors. The Government Accountability Office (GAO) report included the results of an investigation into just how much brain drain the government was losing to the private sector. The investigative arm of Congress reported that some 2,435 former senior officials with the Pentagon had left to work for some fifty-two private contractors.

Just three months earlier, the Congressional Budget Office (CBO) released its own figures about private contractors. The United States was using contractors more than it ever had. In Iraq, they were operating on a one-to-one ratio alongside U.S. troops.

The CBO also found that U.S. agencies had awarded some $85 billion to contractors for work performed in the Iraq theater, which included the countries of Iraq, Bahrain, Jordan, Kuwait, Oman, Qatar, Saudi Arabia, Turkey, and the United Arab Emirates. The Department of Defense had spent $76 billion of that total; the U.S. Agency for International Development awarded $5 billion, followed by the State Department at $4 billion. Another $10 billion had been spent for work performed in Afghanistan.

The CBO tackled another question that had been looming over the industry for years. What was the cost of a contractor in comparison to a member of the military? Were the taxpayers in fact saving money by hiring out, as Prince had long argued? Industry leaders had been boasting for years that they were a cost-saving measure, but they didn't have the data to prove it.

"The costs of a private security contract are comparable with those of a U.S. military unit performing similar functions," according to the report. "During peacetime, however, the private security contract would not have to be renewed, whereas the military unit would remain in the force structure." In other words, there was no savings during wartime, but "demobilization" was a lot faster with contractors: the government could shut down its contracts quickly.

BY JUNE 2008 Prince and Blackwater had caught the eye of Mia Farrow, whose New York–based organization Dream for Darfur was pushing for immediate intervention to stop the killing of innocents. Farrow and Dream for Darfur director Jill Savitt had seen Prince's comments in the newspaper that he could do the job with the numbers of troops already on the ground. They were intrigued. Farrow, who had been to Darfur no fewer than ten times in four years, knew about Blackwater's reputation, but she still wanted to talk to Prince.

Prince, Farrow, and Savitt met for breakfast at a hotel on New York's Upper East Side. Prince knew of Farrow's dedication to the Darfur issue, and he was determined to find a place for his company in stopping the Janjaweed militia. Prince had a detailed vision of what Blackwater could do. He explained to Farrow and Savitt how a 250-man unit could significantly save lives in Darfur. The unit would be made up of highly trained former military contractors who could slap down the Janjaweed threat—but the idea would need the right backing. Prince was convinced that within just forty-five days of getting a go-ahead, one of his companies, be it Blackwater or the less notorious Greystone International, could bring about significant change. He knew that it wasn't only Darfur, but the entire African continent, that provided a wealth of opportunity for companies like his.

"Unfortunately, if you wait long enough, there will be some other place," said Prince. "Sierra Leone will have problems, Ghana had problems, Liberia had problems, Côte d'Ivoire: there's never a shortage of that kind of problem."

Prince suggested putting together ready-made packages of just about everything you would need to provide humanitarian relief after a disaster.

"Pack tents, hospitals, water purification, generators, bridge-building equipment, stuff to turn the lights back on in airfields, so you fly in more stuff," he said. "Cost-effective, fast, simple."

Gary Jackson could also see the company's future on the African continent, from offering security to providing simple infrastructure. "There are fewer roads there today than there were in 1960," said Jackson. "There's a lot of work to be done there." Blackwater already had contracts on the continent for the Department of Defense, providing aviation services to and from various locations, but Jackson also envisioned building windmills to bring sustainable energy to the most remote regions. As Prince sat with Farrow and Savitt, he made his pitch for just how effective his men could be if they could only get into the region, attached to some NGO, for example.

The problem was that while Sudanese president Omar al-Bashir had agreed to allow a peacekeeping force in, he insisted it consist only of African Union troops. There were about nine thousand fit to do the job, and they were only lightly armed.

Prince told Farrow and Savitt that he could train and transform a thousand African Union soldiers into a highly effective force for the Janjaweed to contend with. Farrow raised the obvious objections. There were issues of national sovereignty, among other things, to consider. But Prince had set his mind on doing something to help. He had tried years earlier to reach out to actor

George Clooney, who had also become an outspoken advocate for Darfur. But Clooney never took the call.

Savitt was convinced that Blackwater could offer technological improvements in the region: better satellite images would allow better intelligence about attacks; surveillance equipment could be installed that would detect and warn of an incoming enemy. But Prince really wanted his own men on the ground, and Farrow and Savitt knew it would never happen.

"He's committed, but he also thinks that Blackwater could get into Darfur," said Savitt. "But there is no way. We would never do anything illegal." Prince said that he never suggested breaking the law.

ON THE ONE-YEAR ANNIVERSARY of the September 16 shootings, Erik Prince boarded a plane to Dubai. He was en route to Afghanistan to work out the details of a yet to be announced deal with the Department of Defense that would mean a huge increase in the amount of business he did in Afghanistan. The U.S. government had contracted Blackwater to train and equip the Afghan border police, and they were now finally thinking of expanding the agreement. What had started out as a contract that required fewer than a dozen men would grow to one that called for more than 200. Part of the plan reportedly involved Blackwater taking over a military base dubbed "Lonestar" near the mountains of Tora Bora. The idea was for the company to use the base as a staging ground for moving border police through the training process. The area was still very much a hotbed of Taliban and al-Qaeda activity. There were rumors that the company would also be assisting in some capacity with intelligence gathering, something that Prince wouldn't elaborate on. Running

the base would embed Blackwater deeper within the U.S. government and put contractors even closer to the front line in the
war on terror.

Not long after his trip, Prince got some bad news. The Pentagon officially turned down the armored vehicle Prince had poured
an estimated $20 million to $30 million into developing. It wasn't
a shock; Prince and his top executives already knew it wasn't
looking good, but the final word meant that Blackwater had to
finish the job it had begun weeks earlier: laying off the staff that
had been hired for the project. Forty employees had already been
let go. Another fifty-seven lost their jobs on Halloween. It was
the final blow that would put Blackwater out of the vehicle business. Prince expressed his usual disgust for a contracting system
he thought fraught with corruption and backroom handshakes.

"It's a network of former colonels and generals, and it's nothing less than political and acquisition corruption," said Prince.

Yet it was the same contracting system that had directed more
than a billion dollars his way in less than a decade. The reality
was that while the project's failure was a setback, Blackwater had
grown so enormous that even its loss on the multimillion-dollar
gamble wouldn't stop it.

But the project's failure had another cost. Bill Mathews was
leaving the company. The program had grown under his command, and when it failed, it was clear that there was little left
for him to do. The government's decision not to grant Blackwater the contract for armored vehicles had forced the company to
shut down its manufacturing program, according to Mathews,
who insisted that his friendship with Prince would continue.

"Erik and I can almost be better friends now because Gary
[Jackson] was really stuck between us. I'm glad that will be gone,"
said Mathews.

But it wasn't just Mathews and the manufacturing programs that were gone. With the Fallujah case now turned over to arbitration and the Afghanistan Flight 61 case still pending, Joe Schmitz was leaving the company as well. While Schmitz insisted that he was maintaining a consulting relationship, Prince said that he was just too expensive. Company counsel Steve Capace (the man who knew all of Blackwater's secrets) had also left, and Blackwater was looking for someone new. Cofer Black was also moving on, following in Rob Richer's footsteps months earlier. After four years with the company, Black was doing what many former spies had done in Washington: he was starting his own consulting firm. He wouldn't say whether Blackwater would be a client.

Things were changing dramatically at Blackwater, not only on the executive level, but throughout the company. There were cutbacks in the free food offered at the company cantina, the numbers of company credit cards, and the company-paid BlackBerries that were issued. Prince was still looking for a silent investor, but it was a hard sell in a tough economy. The one business that seemed to be solid was the one Prince had originally set out to do: training.

THE DEPARTMENT OF JUSTICE rolled out the names of the accused in December 2008, fourteen months after the deadly shootings in Nisoor Square.

Donald Ball, twenty-six, of West Valley City, Utah; Dustin Heard, twenty-seven, of Knoxville, Tennessee; Evan Liberty, twenty-six, of Rochester, New Hampshire; Nick Slatten, twenty-five, of Sparta, Tennessee; and Paul Slough, twenty-nine, of Keller, Texas, were facing an array of charges ranging from manslaughter to attempted manslaughter to using a firearm to commit a crime. All of the men had been indicted on fourteen counts of voluntary manslaughter and twenty additional counts of attempt to commit manslaughter. Photos released by the attorneys showed all of the men in military uniforms, from several years earlier. But that's not whom they were working for that fateful day in Iraq.

A sixth guard, Jeremy Ridgeway, had cut a deal with prosecutors and laid out his own account of just what happened on September 16, 2007. Ridgeway pled guilty to the charges of voluntary manslaughter and attempt to commit manslaughter. Prosecutors contended that on or about September 16, 2007, Ridgeway and the others "unlawfully and intentionally, upon a sudden quarrel and heat of passion, did attempt to commit manslaughter." Ridgeway's account of just how so many Iraqis ended up dead that day was incredibly disturbing.

Prosecutors say that it was just around noon when the four-truck tactical support team using the call sign Raven 23 responded in the aftermath of a car bomb. As a support team, they were unaccompanied by any clients and were not busy with any personal security of their own. According to the government, Raven 23 had not been authorized to leave the Green Zone that day, and shortly after doing so, the convoy disobeyed an order by a State Department regional security officer to return as soon as possible. The Blackwater team proceeded to set up a blockade at the Nisoor Square traffic circle, in a busy Baghdad intersection. They entered the square against the flow of traffic and blocked it from entry from the south or west. The team was heavily armed with M-4 assault rifles, M-240 machine guns, 9 mm Glock pistols, and at least one grenade launcher. According to Ridgeway, Blackwater men in the third vehicle opened fire on a white Kia sedan that had been approaching the circle from the south. The driver was a second-year Iraqi medical student named Ahmed Haithem Ahmed Al Rubia'y.

Ridgeway told prosecutors that he heard the initial shots and saw one of his teammates fire a machine gun into the Kia. He could see that there was a passenger in the car as well, and he trained his weapon on that passenger, firing multiple rounds and killing Al Rubia'y's mother. Ridgeway insisted that other Blackwater guards also shot at the vehicle. At least one other Blackwater guard launched an M-203 grenade at the car, causing it to explode. Ridgeway said that the car's driver had been given no warning of punishment for failing to come to a complete stop. According to prosecutors, Raven 23 left the circle minutes later, with turret gunners continuing to fire machine guns at civilian vehicles. At least fourteen civilians were killed in the incident that lasted just minutes.

Ridgeway pled guilty to the charges, admitting that he had fired without any legal excuse or justification. Prosecutors would try to prove that all of the men charged had violated the use-of-force policies of the State Department. They were convinced that none of the victims were insurgents and that many of them were shot while trying to flee the gunfire. The question boiled down to whether or not the Blackwater guards felt they were protecting themselves from grave bodily danger. Lawyers for the accused insisted the charges were simply untrue and were brought after the men refused to plead guilty to what they described as minor charges. For the defendants' attorneys, it was nothing short of a politically motivated case.

There were no charges brought against Blackwater as a company. In fact, prosecutors said that many of the men on that team acted professionally and responsibly. They also stressed that the charges were in no way an indictment of the company, something Blackwater welcomed in a statement that also reiterated its own position on what happened that day.

> *This development does not change our support for those who maintain that they acted appropriately in response to a perceived threat. Blackwater does not have access to all of the information gathered by investigators. Based on the information available to us, however, we understand that these individuals acted within the rules set forth for them by the government and that no criminal violations occurred.*

The case would be an important one not only for the defendants and victims of Nisoor Square, but also for the industry. It would set a legal precedent for how the government might deal with contractors in the future, and would provide proof of whether or not the Military Extraterritorial Jurisdiction Act of 2000 would really apply to them. But Iraqis weren't waiting for the legal landscape in the United States to be tested; they were already enacting their own rules that would lift immunity for contractors from Iraqi prosecution as of January 1, 2009.

They were also kicking Blackwater out. By the end of January, the Iraqi government announced it would not grant the company a license to work in Iraq. The State Department said it had no choice: no license, no contract. Prince found out about it from a blog, and as his anger simmered, he reached out to the department now run by Hillary Clinton to offer a hybrid solution: Blackwater could team up with an Iraqi company to manage the personal security teams working in the country. It was a last-ditch effort to save the business, but the State Department would have none of it. Blackwater lost the most lucrative contract it ever had. It was an abrupt blow to Prince's booming empire. It wasn't necessarily a game-ender for the company, but it was an epic game changer.

Prince was deeply angry at a State Department he considered ungrateful. From his perspective, he had built a machine to recruit, vet, train and deploy contractors in support of their mission, and that was the thanks he got. "Now I know how it feels to have your country turn on you" was how he put it. He was moving even closer now to hiring an outside manager and walking away, and some of those close to him supported the idea. They also supported an expensive rebranding of the company, in hopes of salvaging what business they could. There was no doubt: the name Blackwater *had* become bad for business. In February, Prince signed off on changing the Blackwater name to Xe (pronounced "Z"). As Prince noted, Xe is the symbol for xenon, an inert, noncombustible gas. It was the perfect, nondescript, low-profile name that didn't really mean anything and wouldn't draw a lot of unwanted attention. Days later, Prince made the surprising announcement that he would be stepping down as CEO of the company, and that Gary Jackson would be retiring. Just months earlier, Jackson said they would have to carry him off the property in order to get him to leave, and just days before the announcement, he said he wasn't going anywhere. But Jackson had received a target letter from federal officials looking at a list of potential wrongdoings that included giving Jordan's King Abdullah two guns as gifts during his visit years earlier. Investigators wanted to know what export and other federal regulations may have been violated. (Jackson believed that he hadn't broken any regulations on purpose and didn't talk publicly about the investigation.) With both Prince and Jackson stepping down, the Blackwater era was over.

DESPITE A GATHERING snow storm in Virginia, Prince went running on the morning when the announcement was made. In less than ten years he had gone from a quietly wealthy Navy SEAL whom no one really knew to a man with access to Washington's greatest corridors of power. His companies had handled the bulk of training for U.S. Navy sailors, protected high-level U.S. diplomats traveling through the sill volatile regions of Iraq, guarded the CIA's most secret locations throughout Afghanistan, transported members of the U.S. military by air in Afghanistan and the surrounding region and at the direction of the State Department, even trained foreign forces for police–type work.

While it was the Republican administration that was largely behind the push to privatize the Iraq war, the Obama Administration would also need those private contractors to be able to maintain staffing levels in Iraq and Afghanistan. Despite Blackwater's difficulties, contracting remains a lucrative industry.

While Prince still won't discuss specifics of how much money he's made since 9/11, a quick check of the federal contracts sets the figure at *well* over $1 billion dollars. With a roughly 10 percent profit margin, as Prince himself suggested before congress, that would put him well over $100 million in profits.

Blackwater, in a lot of ways, reflects Prince's own personality: stubborn, driven, and obsessed with finding ways to make things happen. While some champions of the free market system see him as a business genius, others see him as a man with more money than wisdom, more energy than experience, and more determination than is good for him.

Both Prince and the U.S. government have learned valuable lessons in the past decade. For the government, it found that it would be a far more accountable and democratic military power if it kept private contractors removed from the use of lethal force, or at the very least, did its job managing them. Prince learned something very different: his appetite for risk could sometimes be costly and his ambitions could thrust him into positions where he would never be comfortable. Finally, he learned to loathe the media. It was the media that played a large role in the downfall of his company, and he would never forget it.

ACKNOWLEDGMENTS

Even as a career journalist, setting out to write a book is a challenge not conquered alone.

Stefan, Kira, Finn, Ryan, Rita, Michael, Angela, Craig, and Al, you will never have any idea how much I appreciate your support and your love.

I have been incredibly fortunate to encounter people who have supported my passion for telling this story. Richard Griffiths, Tim Lister, Edith Chapin, Jamie McIntyre, Pentagon producer extraordinare Mike Mount, Octavia Nasr, and so many of my CNN colleagues around the world who offered support and encouragement, I thank you.

Thanks to Ken Robinson; my agents Richard Abate, Shawn Coyne, and Brian Lipson; and the incredibly talented Bruce Nichols at HarperCollins. Every author should be so lucky to work with someone like Bruce.

Finally, I want to thank the many I cannot name here. Many of them have requested anonymity, and they have earned my respect for their willingness to tell the truth as they saw it, when many would have rather stayed quiet instead of taking the risk. So much of what I do depends on people willing to trust in the truth.

I lost a colleague along the way, and CNN lost a great journalist. Nancy Coleman, may you always know what a respected and passionate journalist your father, Bob, was.

INDEX

Suzanne Simons is an executive producer with CNN. As a former freelance anchor and reporter, she was based in Bonn and Berlin, Germany, and anchored flagship news programs for both CNN International and Deutsche Welle. In 1999 she also covered the conflict in Kosovo, where she was among the first journalists to arrive at the Pristina airfield as Russian troops refused to yield control to NATO. She has received both the Peabody and duPont awards for her contribution to CNN's coverage of Hurricane Katrina and of the 2005 Tsunami disaster, respectively. She is married with three kids.